Autophagy Secrets

Promote Longevity and Anti-Aging, Burn Fat, and Achieve Peak Performance

with

Intermittent Fasting and Autophagy

Autophagy Secrets

PUBLISHED BY: Mark Evans

© Copyright 2019 - All rights reserved.

The content contained within this book may not be reproduced, duplicated or transmitted without direct written permission from the author or the publisher.

Under no circumstances will any blame or legal responsibility be held against the publisher, or author, for any damages, reparation, or monetary loss due to the information contained within this book. Either directly or indirectly.

Legal Notice:

This book is copyright protected. This book is only for personal use. You cannot amend, distribute, sell, use, quote or paraphrase any part, or the content within this book, without the consent of the author or publisher.

Disclaimer Notice:

Please note the information contained within this document is for educational and entertainment purposes only. All effort has been executed to present accurate, up to date, and reliable, complete information. No warranties of any kind are declared or implied. Readers acknowledge that the author is not engaging in the rendering of legal, financial, medical or professional advice. The content within this book has been derived from various sources. Please consult a licensed professional before attempting any techniques outlined in this book.

By reading this document, the reader agrees that under no circumstances is the author responsible for any losses, direct or indirect, which are incurred as a result of the use of information contained within this document, including, but not limited to, — errors, omissions, or inaccuracies.

Table of Contents

Introduction 4

Chapter 1: What is Autophagy? 6

Chapter 2: Understanding Its Pros and Cons 11

Chapter 3: Ten Ways to Induce Autophagy 22

Chapter 4: Activating Autophagy through Fasting 36

Chapter 5: Intermittent Fasting 41

Chapter 6: The Different Stages of Fasting 49

Chapter 7: Different Ways to do Intermittent Fasting 58

Chapter 8: Long Term Fasts vs. Short Term Fasts 66

Chapter 9: The Effect of Ketogenic Diets 82

Chapter 10: Keto Meal Plan to Boost Autophagy 96

Chapter 11: The Exercise-Autophagy Connection 109

Chapter 12: Deep Sleep and Autophagy 122

Chapter 13: Time Restricted Feeding 128

Chapter 14: Heat Exposure 135

Chapter 15: Hot and Cold Therapy 145

Conclusion 148

Thank you 149

Resource Page/Sources Cited 150

Introduction

Autophagy literally means "self-eating" from the Greek.

It may sound cannibalistic at first but if you consider the fact that it happens in the cellular level then it doesn't sound so morbid. In this book we highlight medical research that has been done that highlights the benefits of this naturally occurring bodily process that promotes self-healing and cellular recycling.

The medical world still doesn't understand how it fully works but we at this point know enough to be able to take advantage of this metabolic process. There are strategies that you can employ today to help you maximize the health benefits from autophagy.

Imagine being able to induce healing at the cellular level. You will enable your body to heal from insulin resistance, burn body fat, repair skin cells, heal brain cells, and a host of other benefits just because you gave your body a chance to let its inherent natural ability to regenerate and heal itself.

This is an exciting field of ongoing study and this book shows you how to make use of present-day techniques to enhance your body's autophagic processes. We will cover the pros and cons as well as a bit of the science behind it. The terms and jargon have been simplified as much as possible so that you the lay person can understand the bodily processes being described.

Thanks for purchasing this book, I hope you enjoy it!

Chapter 1: What is Autophagy?

The word autophagy is derived from the Greek words auto, which can be translated to "self", and phagein, which is translated to "to eat." You put those two together and what you have is that autophagy means "to eat the self"—that sort of sounds macabre to a certain degree.

This "eating of the self" that occurs in the human body is actually more of recycling than actually consuming or digesting one's body parts. Big hint: all of this occurs on the cellular level. It's not like your body's digestive system will go gung ho and start acting on your other organs.

Autophagy and Apoptosis

Autophagy is actually a wonderful thing—it is the body's way of recycling its own broken-down parts. Yes, again that is usually done on the cellular level. The old and worn out machinery of our cells like the cell membranes, proteins, organelles, and such will be broken down and then reused since there is no longer enough energy to sustain it as a part of the functioning whole.

Note that this is not a wild viral thing that happens in the body. It is actually quite an orderly process and it shows how well our bodies have been designed. An old cell that undergoes autophagy is degraded, broken up, and then recycled down to its cellular components.

Another similar bodily process is called apoptosis. Apoptosis means a preprogrammed cellular death—yes, equally morbid sounding as autophagy. What this really is in simple terms is that when the body's cells have undergone several times of cell division it is programmed to die.

It would sound like the body is some huge ingrate getting rid of things after it has gained all the benefits from them. However, that is not the case. Both autophagy and apoptosis are actually beneficial to your very own health.

How is that?

Well let's use a certain analogy—think of a brand-new car. Every cell in your body is like that car. When it was brand spanking new it was efficient and it was very helpful. Of course as the years went by your car gets an oil change, you get it tuned up, and maybe you added some decals and perhaps you even upgraded or customized certain parts.

However, as the years roll by your car gets older and it will get beat up from all the use and abuse you give it. After driving it for more than a decade or two, the maintenance costs for what used to be a wonderful piece of machinery will keep going up.

It was a great car—no doubt about it. It has given you a lot of great memories but it's just that it is no longer beneficial to keep it. It breaks down more than you are driving it since its serviceable life has already passed.

What's the best option for you at that point? It is to sell the car, break it down, and maybe reuse the parts for other projects that the buyer may have in mind. What do you end up with? You get to buy a new car.

The same thing happens to the cells of your body—believe it or not.

But the body's cells are more efficient than we think we know when it comes to these matters. The usable life of each cell has already been predetermined or pre-calculated. After so and so number of cell divisions it has been predetermined that the original cell is already old and clunky.

These old cells are no longer functioning at optimum levels. It costs more to maintain them than to get new ones so the body opts for the better option—apoptosis. That way you don't need to worry about the proverbial car breaking down at the worst possible moment—when you need it the most.

Looking at It at the Sub Cellular Level

Think of autophagy as the process that happens before apoptosis. Autophagy is the maintenance period where the cell can still go on and it just needs replacement for certain parts. If after some time that no longer works then apoptosis kicks in so that an entire new cell will take the place of the old one.

Going back to the car analogy, sometimes all a car needs is a new battery, maybe a replacement spark plug, or some other part and then it will be good to go. This very thing happens to the cells at a sub cellular level. For instance only certain organelles are destroyed so that the cell can make new ones.

The old organelles can then be removed along with the rest of the cellular debris. Do you know what that roughly translates to? It means your body is naturally getting a detox at the cellular level. Now that is what a real detox is – the old and bad parts that no longer function is discarded and thus the working and functional environment of a cell is optimized.

Discovery and Short History

The bodily process of autophagy was first discovered in January of 1962 at the Rockefeller Institute by Professor Keith R. Porter and Thomas Ashford, his student. In their studies they noted that after adding glucagon, they noticed an increased number of lysosomes. Lysosomes are that part of the cell that is responsible for breaking down parts that are no longer needed. It was Christian de Duve, a Nobel Prize winner, who eventually coined the term "autophagy."

More studies on autophagy were conducted in the 90s. One of the discoveries was that there were genes that were related to the process. Michael Thumm and notably Yoshinori Ohsumi discovered starvation-induced non-selective autophagy. Ohsumi eventually was awarded the Nobel Prize in Physiology or Medicine in 2016.

It was in this turn of the 21st century when the field of autophagy research has gained a lot of traction. We don't know everything about it but we are learning a lot. There is plenty of scientific research that have been and are being conducted especially those that are related to cancer, aging, and other neurodegenerative conditions.

Chapter 2: Understanding Its Pros and Cons

Now, even though the name of this bodily process kind of sounds like it is a bad state of affairs, it is a proverbial fountain of youth. From the discussion in the previous chapter we have learned that it is one of the ways the body renews itself from the core of our beings.

There is ongoing medical research on how to use of autophagy as a kind of therapy. That is one of the many uses that experts are looking into. However it should be pointed out that autophagy as a therapy is not for everyone.

It also has downsides. In this chapter we will go over both the pros and the cons of using autophagy as a therapeutic approach.

It May Preserve and Lengthen Your Life

Autophagy as a therapeutic approach may save your life—okay that sounded like something from an infomercial. However, take note that it is accurate, scientifically speaking. It is after all a core mechanism of the body that occurs naturally.

Our bodies enter different states of autophagy at different times and at different degrees. It is a process that your body performs to basically save your life. It basically kicks in when you are sick, when you are in a state of starvation (especially when in a prolonged starvation mode), when you are suffering from an infection, and of course when you are under a lot of stress.

It is used by the body to maximize the repairs that can be done and to ensure minimal damage in case a virus or any invading bacteria or otherwise has come to threaten your bodily systems. Is it possible to induce autophagy without illness or anything life threatening? The answer is yes.

That is best achieved with the help of intermittent fasting. That is the best known way to put the human body in that state of "self-eating." But studies have also shown that adding some fat in intermittent fats as well as other nutrients and other kinds of food can also help boost the autophagy process.

When you do intermittent fasting your body enters starvation mode every now and then. Doing so will also starve an infectious intruder of the glucose it usually feeds on. Since the body's glucose levels go down it also produces another effect—inflammation is also reduced.

Since inflammation is reduced the immune system is given a bigger legroom to do its job since it can concentrate on fighting off the infection instead. In short, autophagy gives your body's immune system an easier time taking action.

We see this in nature a lot of times and we just didn't know it back then. Animals have basically evolved based on their body's autophagy process. When they are sick they conserve energy and refuse to eat. They go into low energy and starvation mode so that their bodies can beat the infection. Well, they don't have medicine after all.

Wild animals also enter this state when food sources are scarce. You can say that it is their way to extend their lives. How does that translate to us humans? Autophagy is a critical part of our bodily systems (particularly the immune systems) as well. When it kicks in you are better able to handle illnesses and researchers have found that it can also help reduce one's risk of developing cancer.

Improves Quality of Life

Autophagy actually has anti-aging effects, which is one of the ways it can help improve your quality of life. It helps to make your skin healthier since the skin cells get renewed, which means newer and younger skin replaces the old skin. However, the benefits of this natural bodily process is not only skin deep.

Recent studies have shown that autophagy improves your overall cellular health. That means every cell in your body can potentially benefit from this process. Remember that it was explained in the previous chapter that autophagy is more like a recycling process.

The damaged parts are taken down and recycled and newer parts of the body's cells are grown in their stead. This same process of recycling and renewal also gets rid of toxic materials that get lodged in the body and it is all done naturally. You can say that this is the body's automatic and natural method for detoxification.

By reducing the toxic damage the body has received you are actually improving your biological age. You may be older chronologically (i.e. according to the day you were born) but you are internally younger physically. The better your body is at repairing itself will dictate how young you really are in terms of biology.

Fine Tuning for Your Metabolism

One of the parts of the cell that gets removed, recycled, and replaced during autophagy is the mitochondria. You can think of the mitochondria as the engine of your cells. They make each cell work as efficiently as they can. Of course just like a car's engine, the cellular engine will also come to a point when it will break down.

Just like an engine, mitochondria burn the body's fuel (mainly fat) and then it produces the needed energy called ATP or adenosine triphosphate. ATP is an organic chemical that gives the cells and the entire body in general the energy that it needs to function.

ATP is used by your muscles so they can contract. They are used by the body for chemical synthesis (i.e. chemical processing). They are also used by your nervous system propagate nerve impulses so that your brain can better control your body. ATP is used everywhere in short.

Now, it isn't that hard to imagine that if the mitochondria has been damaged or plagued by toxins then it gets damaged and/or comes to a point when it can no longer function properly. Thus it will also need to be repaired or recycled and then replaced with a new one. And that is what autophagy is for. It basically gives your cell's engine a tuneup—well it's more of an overhaul actually.

Reduce Risk of Neurodegenerative Diseases

Neurodegenerative diseases are the kind of medical conditions that occur in the brain. They usually don't happen in a day, month, or even a year. They are the diseases of the aging brain and they usually take many years to develop. By the time you know it they have already entered into their full blown state.

They develop that way because it takes many years for proteins that are found around as well as in your brain cells to accumulate, develop, and get mis-folded. In time they eventually don't work the way they should anymore.

Again, researchers believe that it is possible for autophagy to be a big help in this department. In this case the process of autophagy aids in the clean-up of the proteins in the brain that are no longer performing, which helps reduce their build up. This process reduces the build-up of amyloid in Alzheimer's patients. In the case of Parkinson's patients it helps to reduce α-synuclein build up in the brain.

There are researchers who believe that dementia somewhat goes hand in hand with another medical condition—diabetes. When someone consistently has high blood pressure, this state or condition actually prevents the body from activating the autophagy process. That means the cells of people with diabetes and related diseases have cells that are already clogged up.

Inflammation Regulation

The process of self-eating can both increase inflammation and also reduce inflammation. It is important that we put that out in the open. When germs, bacteria, or viruses invade the body, the process of autophagy helps to boost the immune response.

The immune system already has less clutter to deal with so it performs better. This means whenever it is needed, your body's immune system can more effectively increase the level of inflammation in an area of the body as needed.

However, that isn't actually always the case. Most of the time autophagy actually reduces inflammations in the body. The cleanup process clears away any excess antigens (i.e. the proteins that trigger the immune response) thus inflammations are reduced.

Cellular Toxin and Microbial Removal

Remember that the cleanup process that occurs during autophagy is in the cellular level. There are microbes, viruses, as well as toxins that get into the cells. Examples of which are HIV and Mycobacterium tuberculosis. These get dumped out of the cells during autophagy along with the toxins that can produce food borne illnesses.

Muscular Performance

Every time you exercise you create micro tears in your muscles. That means pumping iron or running doesn't really make your muscles more defined and larger. It is the repair that happens after you work out that creates those abs and other well defined and toned muscular features.

It requires energy to exercise so that your muscles can perform how they're supposed to and it also requires energy to repair them when you rest. When your body undergoes a cleanup the cells in your muscular tissues will require energy both when they are in use and when they are being repaired. This balance in the use of energy helps to provide more energy for the repair process of your muscles and also reduces the risk of any future damage that will be made when you exercise.

Preventing the Onset of Cancer

Since autophagy aids in the control of chronic inflammation then it is a big help to prevent the onset of cancer. Research also suggests that it may also suppress other bodily processes like DNA damage response and genome instability that also lead to the formation of cancer cells.

However, this is a double edged sword as one research points out [1]. Researchers suggest that yes autophagy may help prevent the onset of cancer but for those who already have cancer autophagy may not be as beneficial as people may have thought.

As cancer progresses, the cancer cells can also activate autophagy but not to clean up cells. It uses the process of degradation and recycling of cells to obtain their much needed fuel. It is also their way to hide from the body's immune system.

Note that when it comes to this field of study there is still a lot of research that needs to be done. We know that chemotherapy induces damage to cells that are non-cancerous and this will also trigger autophagy.

One interesting subject that researchers are looking into is the comparison of chemotherapy and autophagy as a treatment. The goal is to see if autophagy can trigger an immune response that will attack cancer cells and comparing its effectiveness to treatments like chemotherapy.

Adding Glow to Your Skin

The biggest organ in the body is obviously the skin. It is the organ that is used to represent yourself to the world as it were. And since it is the organ that is one of the organs that are directly exposed to the environment it does take a lot of beating.

The skin takes punishment from environmental conditions, chemicals we apply on it, changes in humidity, and the changing temperatures from heat to cold and back. Oh, our skin also gets physically damaged from bruises, cuts, and other physical injuries.

Now, we know that our skin cells tend to change often due to all of this stress that it goes through. However, toxins still tend to accumulate on our skin and when that happens the skin tends to age. Left on its own it just can't cope with all that punishment. Using autophagy as a treatment may be able to boost the rejuvenation that the skin needs.

Weight Management

The science that purportedly supports the use of autophagy for weight loss isn't completely there yet. There are studies that suggest that it might help people maintain a healthy weight but more studies are required to confirm everything.

Here are some of the factors that lend credence to the use of autophagy for weight management:

- The body's fat burning processes must be activated first before autophagy can be induced. When that happens fat is burned but proteins are spared in the recycling process. However, do take note that if the duration of your fasting tends to get longer, then your body will also begin to lose protein mass. Keeping fasting periods shorter is the way to go to lose unwanted fat and help the body make use of protein.
- Autophagy helps prevent chronic inflammation. It has been observed that chronic inflammation will raise insulin levels in the body. Increased insulin levels then causes an increase in weight. That is why reducing inflammation may help people lose weight.
- Autophagy is all about making your metabolism more efficient again. When the body's cells get that much needed repair the metabolism also gets some fine tuning, which may help the body burn more fat.

Improving Digestive Health

The cells in our intestines tend to do a lot of work albeit constantly. They usually need a lot of repair as well as restoration and autophagy can help boost that process. It will help improve your gut health thus allowing your gastrointestinal tract some time to heal itself.

Not for Everyone

According to the same study cited earlier autophagy can help suppress tumors. However, when the cells are under stress autophagy tends to turn on you. Tumor cells can take advantage of the ongoing autophagy process for them to survive. In this way autophagy is both good and bad for the body. In another study it is suggested that autophagy promotes the survival of the fittest cells of the human body[2].

Again, do take note that the science behind the use of autophagy in cancer treatment isn't completely there yet. There are studies that show that the lack of autophagy in the body can lead to the reduced production of genes that suppress tumors [3]. However, it should be noted that these studies lack actual human trials.

The bottom line here is that promoting autophagy or inducing autophagy is not for everyone. If you have a preexisting medical condition prior to practicing any form of induced autophagy then you should first consult with your doctor before you attempt anything.

Chapter 3: Ten Ways to Induce Autophagy

In this chapter we will go over different ways to induce autophagy. There is no doubt that the best way to bring your body into autophagy mode is to go on a fast. Well basically because that the exactly what the body needs to be in—starvation mode (well sort of).

But fasting and starvation are two different things. We'll go over the itty gritty details about that in the next chapter. In this chapter we will have an overview of the things that you can do to activate autophagy besides fasting.

There are several and natural ways that you can influence it. By doing this you are reaping a host of benefits such as reducing your risk for neurodegenerative disease, inflammation, depression, and other related symptoms.

In this chapter we will go over lifestyle habits, food that you can eat, and other things that can help get your body started on autophagy. However, it should be stressed here that the real best way to induce it is nothing more than by fasting.

You can use the information here and combine it with a fasting regimen in order to better prepare your body to enter into autophagy mode. There is no magic bullet that will work for everyone and that is why researchers, dieticians, and other experts have looked for ways to induce autophagy.

Option 1 – Fasting/Intermittent Fasting

Let's get this one out of the way and we won't go over this in detail because we have an entire chapter on intermittent fasting in this book. Fasting is no less than a biological stressor that solicits a reaction from the body—just like exercise (see details below).

Fasting deprives the body of nutrients and the body will react to that. Studies have shown that fasting can greatly induce autophagy in the human brain as well as in the other organs as well [4, 5, 6].

The challenging part is that you will have to stay fasted for 24 to 48 hours in order to get the highest levels of autophagy and also the best benefits from this metabolic process [7].

The big problem with this is the length of the fast. It is usually not practical and it is not a realistic option for many people. The good news is that there are a variety of fasting regimens that you can try.

You may be able to find a suitable one for you and you can combine that with the other autophagy inducing techniques/methods discussed in this chapter. Remember that studies suggest that even shorter fasts can promote better neuronal autophagy [8].

Option 2 – Exercise

Aside from fasting, another way that you can lower your body's blood insulin levels is through exercise. In fact, this is one of the best methods to induce more autophagy to happen in your brain—where it matters the most.

There are of course different types of exercises and not all of them are better suited to promote autophagy. So, which type of exercise should you focus on? Researchers have found out that aerobic exercises are your best option at inducing autophagy [9].

Resistance training should also be part of any exercise regimen and it will help keep the body healthier. But if you are looking to increase your chances of activating autophagy mode you will focus on aerobic exercises.

Aerobic exercises are the ones that will usually make you pant a lot or pause and catch your breath. People usually call them cardio exercises. Aerobic exercises improve cognitive function and experts believe that this is due to autophagy [10].

Exercise produces stress in the body and autophagy is one of the ways the body copes with stress. Studies suggest that it only takes 30 minutes of aerobic exercise to induce this stress and to trigger a level of autophagy [11].

As a result this metabolic state becomes a huge benefit for overall brain health. It reduces neurodegeneration and at the same time it increases neurogenesis. That is way researchers highly suggest exercise—aerobic exercise especially—for obtaining optimal health for the brain.

You don't have to stick to jogging or treadmills. The idea is to find an aerobic exercise—say swimming?—that you enjoy doing and keep doing it. That way you tend to commit to it thus increasing your chances of success.

Option 3 – Go Through a Protein Fast

According to one study, going through a protein fast has the same effects as undergoing a calorie restriction[37]. How is a protein fast done? You might have to measure your protein intake per week when you do it.

You should first account for all the protein sources that you eat for each week that you plan to go on a protein fast. Yes, you may have to go semi-vegan too. Plant proteins should also be avoided if you have already reached your limit.

So pick a week or two in each month when you plan to go on a protein fast. On your protein fast week(s) pick two days in that week when you will go on your protein fast.

On your protein fast day you have 2 options:

 a. Don't take any protein for that day—both from plant and animal sources (no proteins!)
 b. Limit your protein intake to 15 to 25 grams per day.

Why do you want to do this? Well, it gives your body a protein break. You are giving your body a full day to recycle the proteins that you already have. Are there direct benefits aside from inducing autophagy?

Yes, there are other benefits. First off your cells go on a deep cleanse without getting any form of muscle loss. Another benefit is that it helps promote the reduction of inflammation.

If you are already used to protein restrictions then you can also schedule 1 protein fast day each week.

Option 4 – Try a Ketogenic Diet

Dr. Colin Champ once said that "Ketogenesis is like an autophagy hack. You get a lot of the same metabolic changes and benefits of fasting without actually fasting." A keto diet is one that is characteristically high in fat and low in carbs.

Of course medical experts are referring to healthy fat sources when they say that you should eat more fat. Ketosis is also seen as a way to reduce neurodegeneration [12]. Even though ketosis and autophagy are not directly related (i.e. you can experience one without the other) they usually occur at almost the same time.

In fact ketosis supports autophagy and vice versa. Autophagy also reduces the amount of amyloid beta in the brain, which will be very helpful for people with Alzheimer's disease [13]. Studies suggest that ketosis can help to reduce brain injury[14]. We have an entire chapter on the relationship of ketosis and autophagy so we will deal with subject there in much greater detail.

Option 5 – Exposure to Hot and Cold Temperatures

Studies have shown that exposure to hot and cold temperatures can also trigger autophagy. One study suggests that heat stress contributes to the stimulation necessary to induce autophagy [15]. It is not yet clear how the heat shock phase and autophagy are exactly connected but studies confirm that one thing does lead to the other and it helps in the body's repair process [16].

In some cultures taking a sauna is part of the daily routine especially during the cold months. There are also other treatment modalities such as cold plunges and some even try cryotherapy. Of course before you try any of these treatments you should first consult with your doctor especially if you are at risk for certain medical conditions. We will go over cryotherapy along with how to use hot and cold exposures later in this book.

Option 6 – Deep Sleep

Sleep is the phase or mode where the body heals. That is why getting enough quality sleep is one of the keys of obtaining a state of autophagy. It shouldn't come as a surprise that poor sleep is one of the contributors to poor cognitive function.

Not getting enough sleep, studies say, negatively affects autophagy especially when you wake up intermittently through the night [17, 18]. There is of course the question of which is more important the length of time sleeping or the quality of sleep.

The answer is both length and quality are important. Experts recommend at least 7 hours of quality sleep each night—that means uninterrupted sleep of course. So how do you improve the quality of your sleep? It is done by taking care of your circadian rhythm and also by promoting the production of melatonin.

Researchers have found that there is a connection between the human sleep-wake cycle (i.e. your circadian rhythm) and autophagy. This interconnection plays a role either in the improvement or decline of cognitive function [19].

When we sleep well at night the brain is better able to produce more melatonin. Melatonin is a hormone secreted in a small gland in the brain called the pineal gland. Studies suggest that melatonin can induce autophagy and also helps to reduce one's risk for neuropsychiatric disorders [20, 21]. We will cover how to increase the quality of your sleep in order to activate autophagy later in this book.

Option 7 – Acupuncture

Acupuncture is an alternative healing method that has been around for centuries. An acupuncturist inserts needles in specific parts of the body to produce a reflex reaction. According to one review, studies suggest that acupuncture can improve learning and memory and also induce autophagy [22].

Another study showed that through this process brain cells are protected via the up-regulation of the pathways for autophagy. It is also suggested that acupuncture can help clear the proteins from the brain that are contributory to Parkinson's disease [23].

There is also testimonial evidence that suggests that acupuncture can also help wean people off their psychiatric medication. Note that some antidepressants can be habit forming and this type of alternative medicine can help with withdrawal symptoms.

You should get this alternative treatment from a licensed acupuncturist. Some even suggest that ear acupuncture is a lot better for inducing autophagy in the brain than other types.

Option 8 – Hyperbaric Oxygen Therapy

Hyperbaric oxygen therapy or HBOT is a treatment modality that is used for brain injury. It is particularly useful for the recovery of the central nervous system after it has experienced an injury.

In this form of therapy, patients will be placed in an HBOT chamber where they are made to inhale 100% oxygen. In this chamber the oxygen is no longer transported through the blood's red blood cells. It is dissolved into all the body fluids which allow the oxygen to penetrate deeper where it is needed.

Since the dissolved oxygen is carried deeper, it is better able to reach areas which were previously blocked off due to injury. Oxygen also is now able to reach areas where blood circulation has diminished.

Studies have shown that HBOT elevates autophagy especially in the nervous system [24]. The big downside here is that HBOT is rather expensive and you have to find a specialized clinic that has the facilities to perform this type of therapy.

Option 9 – Foods That Help Induce Autophagy

It may sound counterintuitive to eat certain foods so that you can induce autophagy. Note that there are different levels or types of autophagy depending on the cells that undergo this metabolic process.

The following is a list of different food that may help boost autophagy.

- **Coffee/Caffeine**

Which coffee is better decaf or regular coffee? Studies suggest that both are equally helpful at inducing autophagy [25]. You should be careful about how much and how frequent you take coffee since caffeine in the coffee can disrupt sleep.

- **Green Tea**

Green tea has been found to restore the brain's autophagic flux [26]. The active ingredient in green tea that contributes to autophagy is EGCG (Epigallocatechin-3-Gallate).

- **MCTs (Medium Chain Triglycerides) in Coconut Oil**

MCTs are the compounds in coconut oil that helps to increase ketone levels in the brain and other parts of the body [27]. If you don't like adding coconut oil to your meals you can just take MCT supplements instead.

- **Reishi Mushrooms**

Reishi mushrooms are rich in bioactive compounds. Studies suggest that some of these compounds may contribute to the activation of autophagy [28].

- **Ginger**

Ginger is another nutrient rich Asian herb that also contains lots of bioactive compounds. Some of these compounds have been found to support autophagy [29].

- **Turmeric**

The curcumin in turmeric has been found to be protective of the brain's cells, which also aids in autophagy [30].

- **Thai Ginger**

This type of ginger may be a bit hard to find and it is not actually ginger to be exact. It is a totally different kind of spice. You usually find in Thai, Malaysian, and Indonesian cuisine. Studies suggest that galangal (i.e. Thai ginger) can help boost autophagy [31].

- **Broccoli Sprouts**

Broccoli sprouts contain lots of sulforaphane a phytochemical that may help increase autophagy in brain cells [32, 33].

- **Acai Berries**

Acai berries of course have been made popular by Oprah (or at least that is where I first heard of it through mainstream TV). These berries are rich in antioxidants, some of which stimulate autophagy in the brain[34]. If you can't find acai berries then you can just get some strawberries or blueberries instead—they too have been found to have the same beneficial effects. Blueberries contain Pterostilbene has been shown to help induce autophagy [35].

- **Extra Virgin Olive Oil**

Extra virgin olive oil is rich in Oleuropein a phytochemical that is contributory to the induction of autophagy. It has also been found to help reduce cognitive impairment.

- **Omega-3 Fatty Acids**

Omega 3 acids are of course essential and beneficial nutrients that aren't produced naturally in the human body. They have been found to be helpful in the treatment of many neurodegenerative diseases. They also increase BDNF signaling which enhances autophagy [36].

Option 10 – Take Supplements

There are certain nutrients that can help induce autophagy. The following is a short list of these nutrients:

- **Probiotics**

Researchers have found that the SLAB51 probiotic formulation can help reduce cognitive decline as well as brain damage [38]. There are other probiotics that may also help as well.

- **Ginkgo Biloba**

Ginkgo Biloba is one of the herbs/supplements that is used to treat mood disorders, improve blood flow to the brain, boost attention spans, and increase mental energy. It is even a prescribed herbal medicine in Germany. Its compounds have been found to be helpful for the treatment of dementia and Alzheimer's and also for the induction of autophagy [39].

- **American Ginseng**

American ginseng is another type of ginseng from the Asian variant. Researchers suggest that it may help induce autophagy and reduce mitochondrial dysfunction [40].

- **Vitamin D**

Research suggests that you can induce autophagy by activating the Vitamin D receptor [41]. Other studies also link Vitamin D deficiency with defective autophagy [42].

- **Acetyl-L-Carnitine**

Acetyl-L-Carnitine has been found to have cognitive-enhancing as well as neuro-protective effects. Research suggests that it can help reverse cognitive decline as well as support the functions of the mitochondria in cells[43]. It does that by inducing autophagy in the brain.

- **Vitamin K2**

If you are taking Vitamin D you should also take Vitamin K2 since this vitamin also helps to induce autophagy. In fact these two vitamins go well together[44].

- **CBD**

CBD or Cannabidiol is one of the active cannabinoids that can be extracted from marijuana. Don't worry this one won't make you high. It is actually beneficial and researchers have found that it both activates as well as enhances autophagy[45].

- **Lithium**

Lithium orotate has been found to significantly increase the production of myelin, which improves overall brain health. It does that by enhancing the autophagy in the brain [46].

- **Berberine**

Berberine is usually extracted from a variety of plants. This alkaloid has been found to promote neurogenesis[47]. It also helps to prevent and reduce inflammation. Through these actions berberine is able to help protect the cells of the brain and induce autophagy[48].

- **Rhodiola**

Rhodiola is also known as the arctic root. It is also known as the golden root in Asia. It is actually a pretty popular herb used to increase both mental and physical stamina. It does this by reducing neurodegeneration via increasing autophagy in the brain[49].

- **Schisandra**

Schisandra is a berry and it is frequently used in traditional Chinese medicine. It is traditionally used to improve someone's mood, reduce stress, and it is particularly helpful for women going through menopause.

Studies also suggest that it can also enhance autophagy[50].

- **Resveratrol**

Resveratrol is known to prevent the development of a lot of Alzheimer's and other neurodegenerative diseases. Studies show that it helps brain cells recover and heal after an injury[51].

- **Spermidine**

Spermidine is a compound that can be found in potatoes, pears, mushrooms, chicken, fermented soy, and aged cheese. If eating these foods will ruin your fasting or diet then you can just take it as a supplement. It has been found to be effective in reducing the aging of the synapses of the brain and this compound also helps induce autophagy [52].

Chapter 4: Activating Autophagy through Fasting

Experts say that fasting is the fastest and most effective way to help the body to get into a state of autophagy[53]. How does that happen? Fasting deprives the body of nutrients which signals the body to activate autophagy. When we stop eating the body's insulin levels go down. And to compensate for that drop in insulin drop, the body produces more glucagon. When you have more glucagon it triggers autophagy[54].

Researchers like the award winning Yoshinori Ohsumi and plenty of others recommend fasting (particularly intermittent fasting) as a means to activating autophagy. There are other methods of course, such as the Ketogenic diet for instance, but we will go over those in a separate chapter. In this chapter we will focus on fasting and how you can use it to induce autophagy.

What is Fasting?

Isn't fasting the equivalent of starvation? Well, not exactly—but yes you will starve at one point. The big difference between general starvation and the practice of fasting is control. Starvation is involuntary—you are forced to it due to the lack of food. On the other hand fasting is not—you chose not to eat.

Starvation can lead to severe health problems and even death. Fasting on the other hand is controlled and deliberate and you can stop any time you want. Yes, you will suffer from the lack of food in both cases but you as you can see you have control when you fast.

Fasting for Religious and Spiritual Purposes

People have been fasting for a lot of different reasons for thousands of years now. Some do it for health reasons while others do it for spiritual reasons. Yes, spiritual reasons.

For instance, Muslims go fasting during the month of Ramadan—they fast for an entire month. Catholics on the other hand do fasting every Good Friday and on Ash Wednesday. On Yom Kippur, Jews undergo a six day fast.

Hindus on the other hand have several new moon fasts like the Shivarati, Saraswati, and Puja. Mormons go fasting on the first Sunday of every month. Other religious traditions that include fasting are those from Jainists, Taoists, and Buddhists.

Fasting for Health and Fitness

Fasting as a practice has been around for thousands of years. So, it's not really new. But you don't have to be religious to go on a fast. Fasting is also a practice for people who are not underweight. Some people try fasting to lose weight. Note however, that if you have health issues you should consult with your doctor first before trying any form of fasting.

Bodybuilders in particular have been looking to cut down on body fat through fasting. You see, when the food supply is cut, the body will start to use its stored energy to survive—the stored body fat to be exact.

During fasting you choose not to eat for health reasons—maybe to cut weight, stimulate autophagy for healing, and other reasons. Food is readily available. You will also have a designated fasting period. After the fasting period you will have to eat and thus end your fast.

Some undergo fasting for a day up to several days with medical supervision. Sometimes you will be required by your doctor to fast before undergoing a medical procedure. But that is a different subject altogether.

You may not know it but you actually undergo fasting every night. You've been doing it your entire life. Do you know where the word "breakfast" comes from and what it means?

Break-Fast

This term actually comes from "break fast"—it is the meal that people eat to break their fasting period. You eat breakfast in the morning; that means you were actually fasting as you slept at night. That implicitly means we all fast at night and it is something that we do daily.

However this nightly fast is actually a short term fast usually lasting anywhere from 6 to 10 hours. Some people sleep longer for various reasons. Body builders and people who are sick need to sleep in order to recuperate.

Benefits of Fasting

- ***Weight Loss*** – as stated earlier there are people who undergo fasting to lose weight. Any extra that gets digested and doesn't get used by the body will end up getting stored for later use. That stored unused body fuel is called fat. Since fasting means not eating the body will switch to using fat for sustenance.
- ***Promotes Longevity*** – as you grow older your metabolism slows down. This condition will later lead to a gradual loss of muscle tissue, which is known as sarcopenia. The good news is that fasting helps to speed up your metabolism, which prevents sarcopenia and the degradation of muscular tissue. On top of that fasting triggers autophagy.
- ***Detoxifies the Body*** – nutrient deprivation is interpreted by the brain as a form of stress or threat and it reacts protectively or defensively. The brain starts up its adaptive stress response and that includes looking for alternative sources of energy. The liver is then triggered to produce glycogen as an alternative source. After that the body turns to fat stores—when that happens the toxins in the fat get

released in the conversion process when fat is used as an energy source.

- **Metabolic Boost** – as it was explained earlier, the body gets a metabolic boost when you go fasting. According to one study[55], fasting can boost the body's metabolism by up to 14%. According to another medical study, people who undergo fasting experience an increase in neropinephrine in their blood. This is a neurotransmitter that increases the body's metabolism.

- **Improves Brain Function** – studies suggest that undergoing fasting may help to improve overall brain function. It promotes the production of BNDF or brain-derived neurotrophic factor. BNDF helps protect the brain from degenerative conditions such as Alzheimer's and Parkinson's disease. According to one study, it is suggested that fasting helps to improve memory[56]—this is according to the Society for Neuroscience. Another study suggests that fasting also promotes the growth of new nerve cells[57].

In the next chapter we will go over what intermittent fasting is and its various forms.

Chapter 5: Intermittent Fasting

We have gone over the benefits and also some of the downsides of fasting in the previous chapter. The next question is what is intermittent fasting, how do you use it to induce autophagy, how to go about it, and how to get started with this type of fasting.

What is Intermittent Fasting?

Intermittent fasting is a method of fasting where you cycle between fasting periods and then eating periods. Currently this is one of the more popular diets and weight loss regimens. It has also become quite popular as a method to improve one's health.

Some believe that intermittent fasting is an ancient secret to better health. Believe it or not it has been practiced by human beings all throughout human history. It is secret well because everyone has forgotten about it in modern times. It is actually more of a habit in certain cultures and only noticed in the west. Thus it is virtually forgotten by many people.

People are actually rediscovering this practice. The interest in this mode of dietary intervention spiked sometime in 2010 when Google searches for the search term "intermittent fasting" went up by 10,000 percent. It became an instant fad and it went on for almost a decade.

Note that intermittent fasting can only be beneficial to you if you do it properly. Yes, at times people do it the wrong way. Some people have reported that they have reversed type 2 diabetes with the help of intermittent fasting. Some also credit it for their weight loss. Obviously when you go on fasts regularly you save money and also time since you no longer have to spend money or time buying or preparing meals.

Warning: Intermittent Fasting is NOT for Everyone

Intermittent fasting does carry it with it some dangers. Well, it is fasting and as it was pointed out in the previous chapter, fasting is not for everyone. Intermittent fasting is still a controversial topic despite its proven benefits.

For one thing it entails certain potential dangers for people who are taking medication. If you are a diabetic and you are already taking prescribed medication then fasting intermittent or otherwise may not be an option for you.

But that doesn't mean diabetics can't go on a fasting routine. In some cases the dosages of some of your medication may need to be adjusted so you can go fasting. But in some cases it is just not possible to go on fasting. The best way to find out for a diabetic is to consult with their doctor.

Apart from diabetics, there are also other people who should not undergo intermittent fasting. They include the following:

- Those who are already underweight.

- People who are suffering from eating disorders such as anorexia
- Women who are breastfeeding and those that are pregnant
- Anyone who is under the age of 18 should not undergo intermittent fasting

A Tool for Weight Loss

At the very core of this dietary practice it is actually just a way to give your body a break from processing all the food that you have eaten. Some people eat way more than they really need and fasting can help the body take the necessary time to either clean up the gunk that has accumulated in its systems and also process the rest of the food that is still in the digestive tract.

It also allows the body to use the stored energy that may have been sitting there accumulating. And for some people they have accumulated way more reserved energy than necessary. In a way you are giving your body a chance to burn off those excess fats.

It should be emphasized here also that human beings have evolved through the centuries to include fasting as a part of the daily routine. In some cultures, like in some Native American tribes and other tribal peoples in the world, fasting is a daily experience. Some can even go on only 1 meal a day and they are living healthy lives.

As it was explained earlier in this book we all go through short term fasts each night. That means people can go on shorter fasts that can last for several hours—and there are those who can go on fasts that can last for days without incurring any consequences with regard to their health.

Remember that body fat is nothing more to the body than a type of food energy. It is something that has been stored away for future use. In order for the body to actually make use of that stored food energy is to stop eating.

When you have stored so much food energy it is a signal that you have lost balance, which is what life is all about. Eating and fasting is part of a balancing scale that we need to go through in order to regain our health. Eating is the flip side of fasting that is why when you aren't eating you are fasting and vice versa.

The Role of Insulin in Fat Storage and Use

Insulin is the key hormone involved in the storage of food energy in the body. Usually when we eat we take in more food energy (i.e. calories) than what is readily needed by the body. That is why the body naturally stores that energy away since it isn't necessary at the moment.

Every time we eat insulin levels in our body rises. This helps the body to start storing excess food energy in two different ways or two separate processes. The first one is when carbohydrates are broken down into glucose (a form of simple sugar). These broken down pieces of glucose will be organized into long linked chains which later forms into glycogen. Glycogen is then stored in the muscles (for immediate use when muscular action is required) as well as in the liver.

Note that both the muscles and the liver don't really have a lot of storage space. They can only store so much—remember that glycogen in the muscles is for immediate use. When all the storage spaces both in the muscles and in the liver are already full then this triggers the liver to convert the glucose chains into fat. This process of transforming glucose chains into fat is called de-novo lipogenesis, which literally translates to "making new fat."

Now, the liver also has some storage space for fat but not that much. Most of the fat that gets converted by the liver is stored elsewhere in the body. When the body reaches that phase then the storage space available is much larger than what the muscles and the liver can provide.

In a way, the amount of fat that can be stored at this point is virtually limitless. This stored food energy will be used only when there is no more available glucose or glycogen.

From this we gather that the body has 2 ways to store excess food energy:

1. Readily available food energy stored as glycogen but stored in very limited spaces.

2. Reserve food energy (i.e. fat) that has virtually unlimited storage but this food energy is much more difficult to access.

Insulin is the bodily hormone that is the key to both the creation of new fat and also the body's consumption of that hard to reach stored energy.

Fat Creation Process

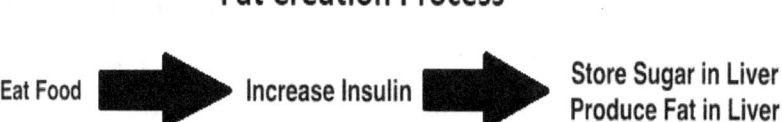

The graphic above shows process 1 where the sugar called glucose is stored in the liver and how body fat is also produced in the liver. Note that this process goes into reverse mode when insulin levels decrease.

Please note the graphic below:

Fat Burning Process

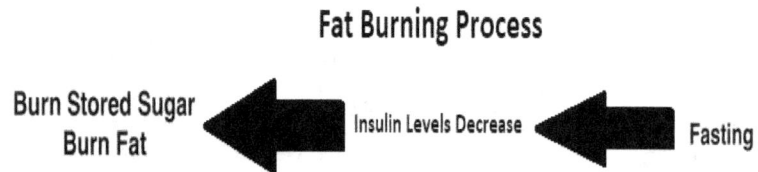

As you can see the process reverses when you go into fasting. This occurs in short amounts or periods every night—except of course if you wake up in the middle of the night feeling hungry and grab a midnight snack.

Remember that the digestive process continues even if you are asleep. Technically you are fasting when you sleep at night whether you had dinner or not. You break that nightly fast if you wake up at 1 am and grab a cookie and then go back to bed.

When you fast and there are no food to digest then the body looks for glycogen—remember the long chains of simple sugars called glucose? Those are the first things that get used up. Glycogen chains get broken up and turned into the simpler glucose which the body can readily use.

If all the glucose gets used up and there is still no food being digested then the body turns to the stored fat. The body will break down fat to convert it into readily usable energy.

From this we can gather the following:

1. The body has two fundamental states.
2. The first state is the high insulin state where you have eaten something
3. The other state is the low insulin state where there is no food in the digestive tract (i.e. you didn't eat anything).
4. Your body switches from one state to the other.

So, if you begin eating the moment you roll out of bed then you trigger the body to enter the high insulin state. And if you stay fed the entire day all the way to the night then you are always in the high insulin state. That is the state when your body is producing fat.

If you continue in that state day in and day out, you are likely going to store more fat unless your metabolism can keep up with the fat production going on. Well, most likely we can't keep up due to the type of diet we have in the modern age.

Intermittent Fasting: Restoring That Balance

Intermittent fasting actually restores that needed balance. It allows your body to switch from the high insulin state to the low insulin state. What you need to do therefore is to increase the amount of time your body spends burning fat rather than making it.

Should you always be in fasting mode? Of course not—that is why you make an intermittent schedule of eating and fasting. There is totally nothing wrong with fasting. It is how our bodies are naturally designed. That's how bears, cats, dogs, and other mammals do it. And that is how we human beings are supposed to do it just as Mother Nature has designed.

Chapter 6: The Different Stages of Fasting

We have just gone over the general steps in the fasting process that goes on when you do intermittent fasting. In this chapter we will dig into the details of fasting in general. Going deeper into these details will help you understand how autophagy fits into the picture.

Yes, we have gone over how the body naturally breaks down glycogen and fat but where and when does it enter into the cellular level? We'll go over that in this chapter.

The Cell Growth Mode

As a kind of recap, when you are in the high insulin state that means that means you are well fed. Whenever you are well fed the cells of your body enter a growth mode. The insulin and something called the mTOR pathway are telling your cells to process proteins and also to cell divide i.e. to grow. Note that when these pathways start to go overactive they tend to help the growth of cancer cells.

mTOR stands for mammalian target of rapamycin. This pathway loves having lots of proteins and carbs. When the mTOR pathway is active in the body it tells the cells not to bother doing any kind of autophagy. That means there is no clean up being done on the cellular level and there is no recycling going on.

The cells are then made too busy cell dividing and growing. They basically have no time to recycle and cleaning up. Thus they end up losing efficiency.

In this growth mode there are different genes in the cells that get activated such as the ones for cell proliferation. When that particular genes get turned on it tends to switch off other genes like the ones used for damage repair and fat burning. That means even at the cellular level your body gets programmed not to burn fat and turn off autophagy when you are in a high insulin state or when you are well fed.

How the Preservation Mode Kicks In

On the cellular level we have a well preserved starvation program. This can kick in when food isn't readily available. Well, not all kinds of food but glucose, yes that simple sugar, isn't available.

We mentioned the mTOR pathway and high levels of insulin earlier and how they trigger the growth mode of the cells. As you might have guessed there is always something that balances something else off. If there is high insulin levels and mTOR, there is also low insulin levels and AMPK.

Think of AMPK as the signaling pathway that steps on the brakes for mTOR. Not only does it make mTOR stop it also signals the cells to enter a self-protecting mode. It also tells the cells to enter into autophagy and thereby start breaking down stored body fat.

Fasting also triggers another internal chain reaction that is related to drinking red wine. Wine has a molecule in it called resveratrol. Now, how is that related to all of this? When you go fasting the number of molecules called NAD+ increases in the body.

Normally NAD+ gets converted due to the presence of proteins and sugars that you eat. Since there aren't any new proteins and sugars coming in the number of NAD+ molecules increase. They accumulate and they become the precursor to Vitamin B3.

Vitamin B3 as part of this chain reaction activates SIRT1 and SIRT3. These are sirtuins, which are proteins that stops cell proliferation (they signal the cell to stop cell division). When the cells stop cell dividing they will turn to other things like the creation of new mitochondria and start the self-cleaning process.

Ketosis Kicks In

When you start fasting ketones eventually are produced in the body. Yes this is another process that goes on when the body isn't busy digesting and processing food energy. It's pretty busy actually come to think of it. The body actually has a lot of other things to do when there isn't a lot of food lining up in its digestive tract. Ketones turn on the body's genes that are related to damage repair as well as antioxidant processing.

Again the trigger here is the level of insulin in the body. That's how the body knows that it has finished digesting food. Now that you have at least some sort of idea what happens in the background when you stop eating and go on a fast, we can now move on to the stages of fasting. We'll be covering fasting in general, which will include long term fasting and intermittent fasting.

Stage 1 – The First 12 Hours

In the first 12 hours of fasting you will enter a metabolic state called ketosis[58]. This is the point when your body starts to accumulate ketones as it was described earlier.

The stored body fat by this time is being broken up bit by bit and then burned or used as an energy source for the body. Some of this fat is used by the liver which continuously produces ketones or ketone bodies. Ketones also serve as an alternative energy source for your brain.

During your resting state the brain uses up to 60% of the glucose that your digestive system is processing. The liver then produces ketones to provide energy to the brain which requires a lot of energy. Ketones are only part of the overall reserve nourishment of your brain cells. Think of ketones as nutritional substitutes for glucose.

There are those who point to ketone usage by brain cells as one of the reasons why you get mental clarity when you undergo fasting. As your brain consumes more ketones the more positive your mood becomes. That is why fasting is so hard during the first few hours because the brain starts to run low on glucose and your grumpiness starts to kick in.

When ketone bodies are metabolized (i.e. used as alternative fuel) they don't produce a lot of inflammatory effects unlike when glucose is metabolized. Another benefit to inducing ketosis is that it kick starts the production of BDNF, the brain's growth factor. The body's repair mode has kicked in well within this phase.

Stage 2 – The 18 Hour Mark

After 18 hours of fasting your body has already switched to fat burning state. Your body is now producing ketones at a significant rate, which is enough to compensate for the lack of glucose. At this point your body fat is now the primary source of energy for your body.

By this time your doctor can perform tests to measure how much ketone bodies are produced by your body. Your doctor can compare it with your baseline values, which should be around 0.6 to 1.0.

When the volume of ketone bodies in your blood increases they can then act as a kind of signaling molecules just like what your body's hormones usually do. Some of the things that ketone bodies signal to your cells include stress stopping pathways, initiate the repair of damaged DNA, and the reduction of inflammations in the body.

Stage 3 – The 24 Hour Mark

At 24 hours into your fasting the cells in your body are now recycling their parts at an increased rate. A lot of repairs are now getting done such as breaking down of any misfolded proteins, which are linked to diseases like Alzheimer's[59]. This phase of brain repair is a huge part of the process called autophagy.

If the human body isn't able to go into a state of autophagy a lot of bad things tend to develop. One of those things is the development of neurodegenerative disease. Since there is no mechanism for tissue rejuvenation at the cellular level misfolded proteins in the brain start to occur more frequently.

Stage 4 – The 48 Hour Mark

When your body operates with very few calories or totally without calories for 48 hours the hormone levels tend to jump up to as much as 5 times when you started fasting[60]. You can achieve this state also consuming very little amounts of proteins and carbs.

Remember that ketones induce the increased production of growth hormones in the brain as well as in other parts of the body. Growth hormones help to preserve the body's lean muscle mass so that your bodily systems do not start feeding off muscle tissue.

Another hormone is secreted called Ghrelin and that too helps to stimulate the production of growth hormones[61]. The production of growth hormones is especially important in people as they age.

Growth hormones are particularly helpful when it comes to maintaining cardiovascular health as well as in healing wounds. Thus experts are conducting further studies on growth hormones suggesting that these hormones may have a role to play in terms of human longevity.

Stage 5 – Insulin Levels Drop to the Lowest Level

This stage occurs around 54 hours into your fast. It should be noted that the body at this point is at its most insulin sensitive level[62]. Note that lowering your insulin levels actually carries with it certain important long term as well as short term benefits.

Apart from helping to trigger autophagy in the body, lowered insulin levels help to make you more sensitive to insulin. In other words you become less insulin resistant, which is something really important to people who are at risk of developing diabetes. Lowered levels also help to prevent chronic diseases related to aging as well as cancer.

Stage 6 – Old Immune Cells get Replaced by New Ones

The next stage in fasting occurs 72 hours into a fast. This can only be achieved through much persistence and practice. No one expects you to reach this level until you have learned how to fast for a few hours first. We will go over how you can properly fast and the different methods that can help you achieve autophagy in a later section of this book.

At this point several signaling pathways that reduce insulin-like growth factor IGF-1 and PKA can now be found in almost every cell of the human body. These signaling pathways help to promote the survival of the body's cells and stimulate growth.

When PKA and IGF-1 are suppressed old proteins as well as old cells get recycled. Prolonged fasting also promotes the regeneration of blood stem cells[63]. Patients undergoing chemotherapy may also benefit from long term fasting as studies suggest. It helps preserve healthy white blood cells.

Stage 7 – Feeding Stage

The last stage of intermittent fasting or any kind of fasting for that matter is the feeding stage. You can't really end a fast without eating again. Every fast must be broken or stopped since the body isn't designed to maintain autophagy for really prolonged periods of time.

The eating phase is just as important as any fasting phase. However it should be noted that breaking a fasting period should be done with a healthy and nutritious meal. That means you shouldn't end your fasting with a ton of carbs. According to the National Institute of Aging, eating a healthy meal after a fast improves the body's insulin sensitivity, promotes synaptic plasticity, and increases the overall resistance of human cells to stress[64].

In the next chapter you will get an overview of the different ways to do intermittent fasting. We will then go over each of them in detail later on in this book.

Chapter 7: Different Ways to do Intermittent Fasting

Intermittent fasting is a blanket term for a lot of fasting methods today. That having said, you should expect that there will be different ways to do intermittent fasting nowadays.

It is no secret that it has become quite a trend nowadays. Some people swear by it saying that intermittent fasting has helped them lose weight. Some credit their extended lifespan to this mode of fasting and others give testimonies as to how intermittent fasting has helped them become healthier.

It shouldn't come as a surprise that different ways to do intermittent fasting have sprung up. Note that there are no hard and fast rules as to how one should do it. However, you should choose the best one that would suit your needs. Not every mode of intermittent fasting will be effective for you. The goal is to make it as effortless as possible.

In this chapter we will go over the common methods to do intermittent fasting. We will discuss each in detail in a later chapter.

The 16/8 Method

The 16/8 method or 16:8 method means that you will fast for 16 hours each day and eat only within an 8 hour window. There are no exact figures but generally you will be expected to fast anywhere from 14 to 16 hours and restrict your eating time to 8 to 10 hours only.

This method of intermittent fasting is known as the Leangains protocol and it was made popular by Martin Berkhan. This is perhaps one of the simplest ways to do intermittent fasting. You can actually get this type of fasting done by just not eating anything after dinner and then follow that up by skipping breakfast.

Let's say you have dinners at 8 you should make sure that you don't have any post dinner evening meals or midnight snacks after that. When you wake up in the morning you should skip breakfast. Let's say you had your dinner at 7 pm and finished it at 8 pm at 8 pm you should refrain from eating anything at all.

The next thing you will eat is lunch the following day. You will skip breakfast, yes. And technically you have already fasted for a total of 16 hours if you do it that way. That is the program for the men. It is recommended that women have a slightly shorter fast, which should be about 14 to 15 hours.

Now this fasting isn't called a dry fast. A dry fast is where you avoid both food and water. That means you don't eat and you also don't drink. Experts say that 24 hours of dry fasting is the equivalent of 3 days of water fasting. Of course dry fasting is going to be a very difficult practice especially if you haven't done any form of fasting.

You can drink water when you go on an intermittent fast. You can also drink some coffee or tea while you fast. This can help reduce the hunger pangs that you feel. However, do take note that you can't take in any alcoholic beverages during your fast.

On top of that during your eating window you are supposed to eat a balanced diet. If you're still eating fast food during the hours when you're supposed to eat then don't expect to see any good results.

Some people do low carb diets in conjunction with the 16:8 intermittent fasting schedule. Whenever you feel hungry during your fasting window then drink water or tea.

The 5:2 Method

The 5:2 Method is also known as the 5:2 Diet and also the Fast Diet. This method of intermittent fasting was popularized by Michael Mosley, a doctor and British journalist. This is another simple strategy where you eat regular meals 5 days a week and then in 2 selected days you will restrict your calorie intake to 500 to 600 calories.

Men are recommended to take in only up to 600 calories during the 2 fasting days. Women on the other hand are supposed to take only 500 calories during those days.

So let's say you want to go fasting on Tuesdays and Fridays. On those two days you will count your calories eating only 250 calories per meal for the ladies and 300 calories for the men.

Critics of this dietary method say that there are no studies that support its effectiveness but we have plenty of people who swear by it. Some don't even consider it as a form of intermittent fasting.

Eat Stop Eat Method

The eat stop eat method will require a full 24 hours to complete. You will also be required to fast two days in a week. This mode of fasting was popularized by Brad Pilon, a fitness expert.

So, how do you do the eat stop eat fasting method? Here's how—let's say you finished dinner on Tuesday and you want to start fasting. You will begin your fast after dinner on Tuesday night. The following day you will not eat breakfast and you will skip lunch. Your next meal will be on Wednesday evening—dinner time.

So, essentially this is a dinner to dinner fast. Note that this is not a kind of dry fasting. You can have water, coffee, tea, and other non-alcoholic drinks during your fasting days. The only restriction is that you should not eat any solid foods.

People use this type of fasting to lose weight. It is also important that you should eat a healthy and balanced diet during non-fasting days. You are not supposed to eat like it's your last meal during the dinner before your fast begins.

That will just defeat the purpose of your fast. You are also not supposed to eat more food during your non-fasting days. It would be as if you are stock piling food for the upcoming fast.

Of course this type of fasting isn't the easiest one to try and it is not recommended for beginners. Note that the drop-out rate for this type of fasting is pretty high and many people will find it very difficult at first. The last few hours before you can eat again will be the most challenging because people usually become ravenously hungry since they are expecting a meal in a few hours.

You don't have to go dinner to dinner if that is not the best option for you. You can do the eat stop eat fasting going breakfast to breakfast or lunch to lunch. You can follow whatever fasting schedule that works for you. Note that this is a challenging fasting method and some people tend to just eat their next meal after the fast rather early.

Alternate Day Method

Now, if you think that the eat stop eat method is tough the alternate day fasting method is even tougher. Again, this is also another mode of fasting that is not recommended for beginners.

Using this method you will be fasting every other day. Note that you will be doing a full 24 hour fast on fasting days.

However, there are also other versions of this fast where you will be allowed to take in around 500 calories during your fasting days. Again that will be 250 calories for women and 300 calories for men for 2 meals.

Note that there are studies on intermittent fasting that have test subjects use this fasting method (or some version of it). The results of course vary for each version. Now this fasting method is not suitable for the long term. No one can keep up with this fasting schedule without feeling miserable. It's a great option if you are looking for healing and rejuvenation but it isn't sustainable. You can have a fasting week once each month but you are already asking too much if you want to do it every single week.

Spontaneous Meal Skipping

This type of intermittent fasting calls for you to skip meals whenever it is convenient. Unlike the other methods for intermittent fasting, this type of fasting doesn't have any structure to it.

In other words you are just skipping meals from time to time. You can just go on fasting when you don't feel hungry come dinner, lunch, or breakfast. You can also just opt to go fasting if you're too busy to cook or you still have a lot of things to do and you don't really feel hungry. Again, in short, you go fasting when it is convenient for you.

You will be surprised that the human body is more than well equipped to skip one random meal any day. You may be traveling and you can't find any food that you like then you can go on a fast until you can find a suitable meal.

You can skip 1 meal or 2 it's up to you and that can still be considered as a spontaneous meal skip fast. That of course falls into the category of intermittent fasting. The only restriction here with this strategy is that you should eat a regular amount for each meal and that you should eat healthy food with each meal.

The Warrior Diet

The Warrior Diet is another popular diet and it was made famous by Ori Hofmekler, a fitness expert. This is a 24 hour fast—well almost since you will have a 4 hour eating window.

In the Warrior Diet you will be eating small meals consisting of raw veggies and fruits. Come night time you will have a feast. You can eat all you can within that 4 hour window at night.

This was one of the popularized diets to incorporate a form of intermittent fasting. Note that this diet also encourages a diet that is similar to the Paleo Diet. That means you can only eat unprocessed foods. The only food allowed is from natural sources.

Note that there are a few common denominators to all of these intermittent fasting methods. One of them is eating regular healthy meals. Another one is that you should shift from an eating phase and a non-eating phase which is why intermittent fasting is a great way to induce autophagy.

Chapter 8: Long Term Fasts vs. Short Term Fasts

There is no question that fasting is the best way to induce autophagy. However, since we have already covered some of the most popular ways to do intermittent fasting, the next question is which is more effective, short term fasts or long term fasts?

These are loose terms actually and there is no governing health authority that has categorized fasts strictly into short or long term. So, just for the sake of comparison we shall include all fasting methods that last 24 hours or less as a type of short term fast and those that require more than that amount of time as a long term fast.

Characteristics of Short Term Fasts

Again, any fasting regimen that requires a fasting period of up to 24 hours will be categorized as a short term fast. Now, when it comes to intermittent fasting there will be a lot of those that will fall into this category.

Note however that we are not saying that there is a best method of fasting. All of these fasting regimens will work for different people and will have varying degrees of success. There is no right or wrong answers when it comes to these things. It sometimes boils down to what works for each individual since each person will have a different health constitution.

Some of the short term fasting regimens will allow low caloric or non-caloric drinks. And there are fasting regimens that fall under the same category that don't allow any liquid intake. That means some fasting methods are dry fasts while others aren't. Both types are still acceptable in this category.

Dry fasts or absolute fasts are the most difficult type of fasting. That is why many fasting regimens today do not incorporate that type of fasting. A dry fast will always be accompanied by some degree of dehydration which may be detrimental to the health of others.

Varying Durations

There are no standard durations for different fasts whether you are talking about long term or short term fasts. Fasts can range anywhere from 12 hours up to a full 3 months. Some fasts require even more time.

You can actually fast once a month, once each week, or once each year. It all depends on the conditions of your health. As it was explained in an earlier section of this book not everyone can fast. There are of course other ways to induce autophagy besides fasting. However, don't expect to get the same results as fasting.

Short term fasts are more suited for people with metabolic diseases such as fatty liver and diabetes 2. You should also work with your doctor when treating more significant diseases via a fasting regimen. Some have found that long term fasting (i.e. those lasting more than 24 hours) can give faster results.

Note also that there is a break in period that occurs for people who haven't fasted in a while. This initial break in period will help people determine which fasting regimen they would prefer. A greater number of people usually prefer short term fasts to long term fasting. However, you can engage in a long term fast every once in a while.

12 Hour Fasting Method—The Original Daily Fast

The 12 hour fast was the way everyone fasted for hundreds of years. There are also versions of the old 12 hour fast today. Just like many short term fasting regimens, the 12 hour fast is expected to be done routinely every day. This one as it was described earlier happens every day when we go to sleep at night.

Everyone had their dinners around 7 pm and then they went to bed. Everybody then woke up 12 hours later and had breakfast. That used to work for everyone for centuries. There was no such thing as obesity back then—well at least it wasn't common. However, something changed.

The change happened in the 1950s when the meal standards changed—actually, it was the standard meal that changed. There came an influx of high carb foods into the standard diet. On top of that the meals were also formulated so that there will be less fat in the everyday diet for most people.

The other thing that changed was the frequency of the meals. Yes, we human beings didn't use to eat 3 square meals a day. No we didn't. As soon as we changed the frequency of meals eaten in a given day it reduced the frequency of our fasting periods.

The 12 hour fast would have still been quite alright even today but there are a lot of things that you should change. You need to remove all processed foods in your diet. You should also avoid excessive amounts of sugar in your diet. On top of that you shouldn't have any significant insulin resistance to begin with. However, given what we have in our meals today the 12 hour fast would not be enough to reverse a lifetime of insulin resistance.

16 Hour Fasts

Another short term fast strategy is the 16 hour fast. You will have 16 hours of fasting each day and that would mean that you will skip breakfast. We have covered the details about this fast in the previous chapter. Yes, this is the one known as the 16:8 fasting.

Martin Berkhan, a pro bodybuilder, wrote about it extensively in his blog which made the fasting regimen quite popular while he was out promoting it. He blogged about it from 2007 to 2010. However, it kind of lost steam and you don't hear much about it from Berkhan through his blog since then.

However, his website is still around which means Berkhan may be off to other forms of business other than just promoting his book and his fasting regimen. You can check him out at his blog at www.leangains.com to see updates. Last time I checked he was taking clients with whom he works with one on one.

I guess nowadays Berkhan is just content letting his books do the talking and he gets to demonstrate his unique concepts about intermittent fasting directly to clients. It would appear that the lean gains diet or 16 hour fasting method works quite well even for bodybuilders. For more information on how his diet works you can check out his book or sign up for one of his coaching sessions.

20 Hour Fasting

The 20 hour fast is otherwise known as the Warrior Diet, which we also mentioned and covered somewhat in the previous chapter. As it was explained earlier, this is a one meal a day fast. Well, not exactly one single meal. It's a one big meal and several tiny meals.

With this diet or fasting system your insulin levels are bound to spike only at night when you have that one huge meal. For the most part during the day your insulin levels will drop down and trigger fat burning and also autophagy i.e. the body's repair mode.

This diet and fasting regimen became popular in 2002. It stresses that the timing of the meals is just as important as the amount of the meal, which is really important when you do intermittent fasting. In other words when you eat is just as important as what you eat. Both elements are equally important.

Hofmekler, the guy who popularized this diet, drew upon the diets of ancient warrior societies like the Spartans and the Romans. During the day even though you are allowed some snacks you will still have to eat unprocessed foods. On top of that you will have to do some intensive physical training to make the most of the calorie burn and fat burn that will be going on for most of the day. The snacks are only there to help you get over the hunger pangs and nothing more. It wouldn't be hard to imagine that this short term fasting method would work for busy people and those who tend to travel a lot.

Are Short Term Fasts for You?

Note that whatever type of short term fast you choose they all have one singular point to everything. They all allow insulin levels to go down during the day (or for a specified amount of time) more than the usual time it goes down when you go to bed at night.

Doing these short term fasts tends to break the insulin resistance that we all feel due to the type of diet that we have in our modern society. The goal of course is to allow the body to reach a state of homeostasis.

Short term fasts seem to be more favorable for more people. Well, the human body is a thing that prefers narrow range events and activities. Any stimulus or activity that is prolonged is usually something that becomes uncomfortable and the body would most likely try to resist it eventually.

Prolonged periods of high level insulin in the blood will result in insulin resistance. The same is true, staying fasted for too long will also be detrimental to your health. What do you think will happen if the body runs out of stored fat?

That is why for most people short term fasts is the way to go. However, if you are looking to treat insulin resistance on a much better scale then a long term fast will be better for you (yes, something that can last more than 24 hours).

Characteristics of Long Term Fasts

Long term fasts are those that last longer than 24 hours. Note that the 24 hour limit is only arbitrary. There is no actual standard that divides which type of fasting is long term and what type of fasting is short-term. Some might feel and believe that 24 to 48 hour fasts should be included in the short-term fasting category.

Fasting for 72 hours is already pushing yourself to a higher limit and your body will be resisting the effort a lot by that time. On the other hand, with some practice, a 24 hour or even a 48 hour fast will seem doable for those who have been fasting for quite a while.

Note that long term fasting should be done less frequently. The actual duration of a fast will usually be up to you. If you can only do 12 to 18 hour fasts for now then stick with that fasting regimen. There is no need to force yourself to fast for longer hours especially if you have a preexisting medical condition.

After fasting for quite a while you will notice that your hunger pangs will increase significantly on day 2 of any fast. Any amount of fasting on day 1 can be bearable. You will find a way to tolerate it as well as you can. But as soon as you reach day 2 the temptation to reach out for food will become quite strong.

It's anywhere from day 2 to sometime in fasting day 3 when hunger and desire for food will be at its peak. After that your hunger pangs will gradually decrease. This is important to know since it will make or break the effort. At least you know what to expect when you undergo a long term fasting.

24 Hour Fasts = Long Term Fasts? Really?

There are people who consider 24 hour fasts as long term fasts. Well, if you haven't done any fasting then not eating for 24 hours will seem long term. That is why I recommend that you start with at least an 8 to 12 hour fast.

Again, take note that you aren't going around with no food in your belly in a 24 hour fast. Let's say you ate breakfast today and you want to start fasting afterwards. What happens is that this breakfast will be the last and only meal you will be having today. You will then skip lunch and also dinner. The next time you will be eating will be during breakfast the following day.

The same thing holds true if you do your fast lunch to lunch or dinner to dinner. Now, some may have already noticed that this type of fasting is kind of similar to the Warrior Diet that we talked about earlier. If you try the 24 hour fast you should count exactly how many hours you haven't been eating. Sometimes you may have to move your breakfast (or whatever meal you had last time) an hour after.

But why stick to the 24 hour or longer starvation period? Well sometimes it's just 20 hours and that will still be fine in some instances.

Now that is a good question. The goal here is to ensure that your insulin levels go down significantly to make your body switch from burning glucose to burning fat. For people who have more insulin resistance. That means the longer the fast the more effective it is. Yes, you may get some benefits from short term fasts but the impact won't be the same as the ones you get from long term fasts.

Note that when you do 24 hour fasts you will still be eating. This is advantageous for people who need to take medication. They can take their meds during their eating window. So for instance, you can take your aspirin, iron supplements, or maybe metformin with the one meal you are having for that day.

Another advantage of 24 hour fasts is that they are easier for people who go to work. They can be incorporated into your daily life. Some people prefer to have dinners as their one meal for the entire day. That way they can still share a meal with their family at the end of the day.

Note that you will not go hungry during long term fasts because you can still have beverages all throughout the day. You can have a cup of tea or coffee in the morning to get you started. You can skip lunch or just have another beverage for lunch. You can spend your lunch time continuing your work with a cup of your favorite drink as you work.

Now, you don't have to do 24 hour fasts every day. Remember that long term fasts should be done with less frequency. Only short term fasts should be done on a daily basis. The maximum for any long term fasting should be 2 to 3 days a week.

Will you lose muscle mass when you do long term fasting? There are studies on this very subject and none of them have reported any loss of lean muscle mass in people who fasted in the long term. In fact, in one study test subjects fasted every other day (i.e. alternate day fasting) for 22 days. Their body weight steadily increased but their lean muscle mass stayed the same.

Slow Rise in Popularity

You would think that with all the hype about fasting in the late 2000s that it would have become quite popular since then but the fact is that it didn't. Sure pioneers like Brad Pilon and Martin Berkhan saw some success but their marketing efforts didn't prove to be quite viral.

It was not until Michael Mosley's 5:2 fasting approach when fasting started to hit the mainstream media. The big difference is that Mosley was a TV producer apart from being a physician. His programs on BBC put fasting on the health and fitness roadmap globally.

Mosley appeared in TV program called Eat, Fast, and Live Longer. Apart from the documentary show on BBC he also published a book called The Fast Diet. Fasting as part of a dietary regimen became a hit sensation gaining intense interest from the public especially in the UK.

Mosley's book became a best seller in the UK of course and then he came up with follow up books as well.

Scientifically Backed Fasting Diets

Mosley's 5:2 fasting diet of course wasn't backed by science although there is already medical research on fasting in general. Greater interest in the form of clinical studies will later follow after the link between autophagy and fasting will be made in later years.

So, which fasting regimen has the most research behind it?

That would have to be Alternate Daily Fasting. The bulk of the research on this dietary regimen was conducted at the

University of Illinois in Chicago with Dr. Krista Varady leading the team.

She wrote about it and published a book entitled The Every Other Day Diet but the book wasn't a big hit, which is a shame. Well, because the diet itself is backed by actual scientific studies. That means the recommendations that Varady made in her book/dietary fasting method is proven to work. Perhaps she needed a better marketing strategy which would have made her book a much better success.

Risks and Complications

Long term fasts are actually better at inducing autophagy than short term fasting. However, long term fasting also comes with its own risks and complications. The benefits do accrue the longer you fast but be aware that there are certain dangers associated with fasting longer, which is why long term fasts should be supervised by a medical professional.

Doctors may recommend long term fasting regimens for people who have obesity that are harder to treat or type 2 diabetics. Nevertheless, you should also be aware that these doctors will also closely monitor these patients, doing the blood work, checking their blood pressures, and checking for other factors.

Note that if at any time you feel sick during your fast then that is a clear signal that you should stop fasting. Fasting should still make you feel healthy and well.

Doctors should also closely monitor your medication intake. This can be a major issue for diabetics who undergo fasting regimens. Those who take the same dose of diabetes medication while fasting run the risk of hypoglycemia. That can be quite a dangerous condition if it all comes to that, which is why your doctor will keep a close eye on diabetics as they fast.

Your blood sugar going down is not really a complication. That is actually what you want to achieve when you go fasting – make your blood sugar drop. However, when your blood sugar is already low and you still take your usual dosage of meds then that may cause some problems. It also translates to the fact that you are already overmedicated at that point, which is why your doctor should adjust your prescriptions for your fasting days.

The dosage of diabetic meds should be reduced and the schedule of intake of certain drugs should also be adjusted. Note that there are medications that can cause an upset stomach when taken without a meal. Examples of such drugs are metformin, iron supplements, ASA, and NSAIDS.

36- and 42-Hour Fasting

If you really want to try going without food or drink (or mainly just solid food) then you can try a 36 hour fast. In many clinical practices patients with type 2 diabetes may be recommended to undergo a 36 hour (or longer) fast for 2 to 3 times a week.

This type of fasting usually produces better compliance among patients and it brings results faster. 36 and 42 hour fasts are better for diabetics due to their higher insulin resistance. This type of fasting regimen has been observed to be much better than shorter but more frequent fasting periods. But that doesn't mean shorter fasting protocols don't work—they do but they don't bring in results as fast as long term fasting.

Is it possible to fast for 42 hours or longer?

A 42 hour fasting routine can be easily incorporated into your daily grind. It's a lot easier than you think. However, remember that this type of fasting should be carefully supervised.

If you are used to having a quick breakfast maybe just some coffee or some other drink to get your day started then this kind of fasting strategy might just suit you. If your mornings are a rush and you usually don't have time for breakfast in the morning then this might just be the fasting habit that will work for you.

That is exactly what you will be doing in a 42 hour fast. You will make it a daily routine to skip your regular meal in the morning (aka no more solid breakfast). The entire morning still counts as part of your total fasting hours.

You will then break your fast at noon time. It is important not to binge eat during lunch as it will ruin the purpose of your fast. If you notice this is the setup for the 16:8 fasting regimen. Yes, it is a short term fast.

What you need to do now is to add a bit of long term fast in between those regular daily fasts. What you can do is to combine that with a 36 hour fast. So let's say you're already used to skipping breakfast having only your regular coffee and water in the morning—you're already doing that 7 days a week Mondays to Sundays.

Let's say you want to do a 36 hour fast on Tuesday. So, you will skip breakfast as usual on Monday and then have your regular lunch and dinner. Come Tuesday morning you will skip everything from breakfast to dinner—essentially living on a liquid diet the whole day Tuesday. The next meal you will be having is on Wednesday at lunch time. Count the number of hours you fasted during that time and you will have done a 42 hour fast.

It is important though that you should not implement any calorie restriction during actual meal times. A lot of times those who have made fasting a daily habit would lose appetite. The ideal thing to do rather is to eat until you are satisfied during your eating period. Eat to satiation not until you can't eat any more.

Why Do Appetites Decrease During Long Term Fasts?

There is a good reason why people start to lose appetite during long term fasting. As your body starts to break its insulin resistance cycle, the usual high insulin levels in your blood decreases steadily.

Insulin is the hormone that regulates BSW or body set weight. If the insulin levels are usually high then the regular BSW is also high. That means your body will want to gain weight i.e. you will get hungry plenty of times.

But when your body breaks its insulin resistance cycle the insulin levels go down. Since there isn't a lot of this hormone in your blood then there will be fewer hunger pangs triggered. In essence, your body wants to go down in terms of BSW. At the same time as your appetite goes down, the body's total energy expenditure also goes down and is better maintained.

Chapter 9: The Effect of Ketogenic Diets

Is it possible to trigger autophagy through a ketogenic diet? If you remember in a previous discussion in this book we talked about ketosis as one of the phases that will be reached on the way to autophagy. How long a fast does it take to induce ketosis and autophagy? Those are the two questions that we will cover and more in this chapter.

Ketosis and Autophagy

Keto diets and fasting diets are some of the health trends today. These are not fad diets since both of them are backed by actual scientific studies. On top of that there is a lot of testimonial evidence for them as well.

Many people have tried them some under the supervision of a physician or some other health worker—like a fitness coach for instance. People do it for different reasons. Some do it for weight loss, some do it for their overall wellbeing, and many people are on these diets looking to resolve or address their individual health problems.

Experts are beginning to understand the role of fasting and ketosis to deep internal healing in the body through both of these diet regimens. *But, what is the difference between ketosis and autophagy?*

We have already established that autophagy is the body's process of recycling cellular parts and it occurs when the blood insulin levels go down. That basically happens when you enter into starvation mode.

Ketosis on the other hand is a metabolic state (which is what autophagy is too) where the body produces more ketone bodies and makes use of them a lot more than usual. As it was explained earlier the liver produces more ketone bodies when the body's glycogen stores are depleted.

Ketone bodies are used as a substitute for glucose. There are two ways to induce ketosis. The first way to do it is to go on fasting. The other way to do it is to go on a ketogenic diet—a diet which is essentially low carb.

Note that autophagy and ketosis are metabolic states that support one another. However, it should also be pointed out here is that these two states or bodily processes are not inclusive of each other. That means you can go into a state of ketosis but never reaching the point of autophagy. The reverse is also true that you can also be in a state of autophagy without essentially be in a ketogenic state.

However, a lot of times ketosis and autophagy accompany one another or occur at the same time because they both follow the self-same principle.

Will Autophagy Require a State of Ketosis?

The next question is whether or not a state of autophagy will require a state of ketosis? We know that ketosis will occur first before autophagy sets in. The key here is to understand what regulates both of these metabolic states.

What Regulates Ketosis

Your body achieves a state of ketosis via glucose restriction. The primary mechanism or driving condition that causes a state of ketosis (i.e. the creation of ketone bodies in the liver) is the depletion of glycogen in the liver.

A deficiency in carbohydrates can also cause the increased production of ketone bodies. Is there anything that can cause carb deficiency in the body? Well, we know that protein can help increase the synthesis of carbs. It happens through a process called gluconeogenesis.

Note however that gluconeogenesis is a secondary factor in the production of ketone bodies. That means this process doesn't affect ketogenic production that much. This also means you can achieve ketosis without having to lower your blood insulin levels—but lowered insulin levels do tend to happen.

That means you can eat food that is rich in protein and achieve ketosis. However, since the calorie content of that food will still maintain the insulin and mTOR levels in your body then you don't achieve autophagy.

What you have achieved is something called nutritional ketosis. In this state your mTOR signaling factor will still be high. That factor will inhibit the state of autophagy. Note that the reverse is also true—you don't need to enter a state of ketosis in order to achieve autophagy. You can be in a state of autophagy for several days and still not achieve ketosis.

How is that possible? It all depends on how keto adapted a person is. But it should be emphasized here that being in a ketogenic state already meets a lot of the requirements to induce autophagy.

In other words even if you are unable to achieve autophagy yet, getting into a state of ketogenesis is already one huge step forward. Some of these requirements include lowered mTOR levels, low levels of blood glucose, and reduced blood insulin. You just need to make a few adjustments in your dietary regimen (e.g. make adjustments in your fasting or include fasting in your regimen).

Measuring Ketone Levels to Estimate Autophagy

There is actually no exact way to measure autophagy in human beings. The studies that have been conducted where a state of autophagy has been determined were largely done on rats and other animals as test subjects.

What we really have are close enough estimates. What your doctor will do is to check your insulin to glucagon ratio and also look at your glucose ketone index. That's as close as we can get at the moment but that doesn't mean we may not be able to find a viable way to measure autophagy. There is still a lot of research going on and this is one of the interests in the ongoing studies.

Experts estimate that it takes anywhere from 48 to 72 hours of fasting to activate autophagy. However, there is no actual timeline and we currently do not know for sure when autophagy has already been achieved.

The length of time needed for fast to induce autophagy depends on the actual nutrient status of the person who is fasting. That is why it will be different from one person to the next. We don't have the means to exactly point out whether the current mTOR and insulin levels have become low enough to achieve that metabolic state.

Key Factors to Consider

There are several indicators that will be considered when estimating the instance of autophagy in human beings. They include the following:

1. When the insulin to glucagon ratio is lower this it indicates that there is nutrient deprivation, fat oxidation, gluconeogenesis, ketogenesis, and more catabolism.
2. A lower score on the glucose ketone index will indicate more AMPK and higher ketosis. This index indicates the insulin to glucose ratio in the body.
3. Higher insulin to glucagon ratio on the other hand will indicate nutrient storage, elevated blood sugar, higher insulin levels, and a lot more anabolism.

The actual length of the fasting period before autophagy finally is induced will be determined by the body's nutrient status. The presence of certain nutrients like ketones, glucose, and amino acids will be telling.

That means if you do not take in too much protein or carbs on a daily basis then you are better poised to enter into autophagy compared to someone who does. That is because you no longer have to burn through a lot of calories to get to that point.

Here's how the glucose ketone index formula is computed by your physician:

1. Your blood glucose is measured
2. The blood ketones are also measured
3. The amount of blood glucose is then divided by 18
4. Divide the result with the number of ketones that was measured in step 2

NOTE: if you are measuring the glucose ketone index (GKI) in mmol/L then you should do step 3. However if you want your figures in mg/dl then your doctor will skip step 3.

Entering Autophagy While in a State of Ketosis

As a recap, remember that the most effective and also the most natural way to enter into a state of ketosis and autophagy is of course through fasting. However, it should be stressed here that you should fast for several days in order to induce your body to enter into these metabolic states. The goal behind it all is to cause energy depletion in the body, which will ramp up the production of ketone bodies in the liver.

Studies have shown that in order for ketones in the body to be synthesized, you will have to enter into a state of autophagy[65]. This is one of the interesting connections between autophagy and ketosis. Gluconeogenesis is not affected by the reduced production of ketones in the liver.

What does that indicate? It means that autophagy is essential if you want to achieve ketosis. It is also an essential state that the body should enter into in order to become more keto adapted. If there is not enough autophagy going on, then the body will stay in a sugar burning state.

According to another study, ketosis actually promotes a different type or level of autophagy called brain macro autophagy. This is accomplished by activating Sirt1[66]. That strengthens the connection between these processes that goes on in the human body.

Ketone bodies also play another role when it comes to autophagy. They help to stimulate CMA or chaperone mediated autophagy. This particular metabolic state will usually make use of specific types of substrates as well as certain amino acids[67].

This gives us a huge impetus for elevating the levels of ketone bodies in our systems since they are very beneficial to our overall well-being. There are two ways to elevate the ketones as well as the Beta-hydroxybutyrate in the human body. The first way as you might have guessed is to go fasting forcing your body into starvation mode. The second way to do it is through eating a ketogenic diet.

We all go through ketosis naturally, just a bit of FYI. It isn't something special that you have to induce. It is not a reserved state of the body that only gets activated in the rarest occasions. People go into ketosis at certain times during the cold winter months.

We also enter this metabolic phase when we eat more protein than carbs. Well, people tend to eat more meat during winter season. The combination of limited carbs, calorie restriction, and larger protein intake makes the body more flexible since it is not restricted in its diet. This combination also allows the body to better activate autophagy and therefore it is much better suited to entering into ketosis.

CMA: Ketosis Providing Support for Autophagy

Eating a ketogenic diet will definitely bring your body to a state of ketosis. When your body is in that metabolic state it can provide a lot of support for autophagy state or phase. That means your body's cells are better able to recycle and repair the needed parts including specific types of protein. This is called chaperone mediated autophagy or CMA.

Do you need to go on fasting to enter CMA mode? Well, not necessarily. The important thing is to keep the protein and carb intake really low for a sustained amount of time. This is one way to allow your body to enter into ketosis while in a ketogenic diet. That way your body can remain in ketosis as it recycles specific types of protein.

If you aren't to eat a lot of protein and you're not going to consume carbs that will fuel the production of glucose in the body, what should you eat?

The answer is that you should eat healthy fats. This is one of the modalities seen as a way to decrease neural injury in patients that have been experiencing seizures. In a way it mimics a lot of the aspects of a body's physiology when there is lowered mTOR and insulin.

Certain fats like coconut oil as well as MCT oil can help increase the body's production of ketone bodies. The only downside is that including too much healthy fat in your diet can ruin your fast since fats are calorie rich and they contain a lot of macronutrients. In other words they can still raise your insulin and mTOR levels if you have too much.

In that case what does a ketogenic diet look like?

The ratio of therapeutic macros in that kind of diet will have to be 5% carbs, 15% to 20% proteins, and 70% to 80% fats. This will help you maintain a keto diet and help achieve autophagy. As you can see you can eat a little more proteins or fats and still stay within a ketogenic ratios.

Now, here's an important detail about all this. You can eat more protein and also more carbs and still stay within ketogenic limits. With that sort of percentage in macros your body will still produce more ketone bodies. The downside is that exceeding those limits will already break your fast.

Which is Better Ketosis or Autophagy?

A ketogenic diet may be low in carbs but it does look like it is a doable diet, right? You won't get hungry due to the amounts of healthy fat that you will be consuming. If you check out keto recipes and keto meals they still look like the regular food that you eat, which means it won't feel as restricting as other diets.

That is why some ask if ketogenic diets can be a better alternative to fasting when it comes to producing the desired effects. Effects would be repair and recycling of the body, rejuvenation, anti-aging effects, etc.

Again, there should be no question about it that autophagy is way better than ketosis when you're looking at health and metabolic benefits. That is if you compare fasting induced autophagy versus keto diet induced autophagy. The level of metabolic benefits from fasting far exceeds the benefits from a keto diet thus fasting wins almost every time.

However, there are instances where a ketogenic diet is better suited for people who struggle with weight loss issues, insulin resistance, seizures, and diabetes. Now, here's a big tip – you can magnify the health benefits of a ketogenic diet by adding some intermittent fasting in between. If you want to maximize the benefits of a ketogenic diet then you should incorporate an extended fast every now and then into your dietary schedule.

Instead of thinking which one is better, the better thing to ask is how you can combine both of these regimens in order to reap the most benefits. A low carb keto diet that doesn't overdo the amounts of protein is a great basal template that you can follow.

It will help you maintain better metabolic health. It also primes your body to go into autophagy a lot faster—that means you don't have to fast too long to enter into autophagy.

So, What Foods Can You Eat On A Keto Diet?

Here is a sample list of foods that you can eat while on a keto diet:

- Cauliflower, zucchini, spinach, and other low carb veggies
- Eggs – note that they are absolutely low carb
- Shellfish and fish – both are also low carb and they are good protein sources
- Meat from grass fed sources – the goal here is to get high quality protein sources
- Yogurt and cheese – high calcium and high protein options
- Butter and cream – these foods barely have carbohydrates in them
- MCT oil, Coconut oil, and olive oil
- Avocadoes
- Seeds and nuts

If you are interested in finding out all the food that you can eat while on a keto diet, we have a list of those foods at the end of this chapter.

2 Important Benefits from a Keto Lifestyle

Researchers attribute certain health benefits from a keto lifestyle. The two most important benefits they cite are the following:

- **Weight Loss** – a lot of people go into a keto diet in order to lose weight. People lose weight for different health reasons. Some need to lose weight because that will help them cope with diabetes. Others lose weight for cardiovascular health. A keto lifestyle is appealing because it helps make the body more efficient at burning fat. You remain full in the process even though you only consume fewer calories. People who suffer from epilepsy have shown great improvements after undergoing a keto diet. It induces the body to produce ketones as well as decanoic acid which are beneficial for preventing seizures.
- **Improved Insulin Sensitivity** – again a keto lifestyle is a huge benefit for people with diabetes. Other than helping these people lose weight they also become more insulin sensitive. A keto diet can lower blood sugar levels.

Safety Issues

The next question that people ask if the keto diet is a safe diet. It is important to point out that this kind of diet does pose some risks. Putting your body in a state of ketosis also has downsides too, which you should know before you jump into it.

Here are some of the side effects of a ketogenic diet:

- Lowered blood sugar levels (this condition may be a problem for some but a benefit for others)
- Indigestion
- Constipation
- Bad breath

The first few days of trying a keto diet can be a quite challenging due to an overall feeling of being sick even though you are eating perfectly healthy meals. Some people experience some form of insomnia while on a keto diet while others report feel nauseous. There is also a risk for potential dehydration and since you will be eating more meat, there is also that chance of developing kidney stones.

Should You Go On a Keto Diet?

Note that no one really knows today what the long term effects of a keto diet are. And that is one of the things that everyone should consider before they try it. It is still best to ask your dietitian or your family doctor before you embark on any dietary change keto or otherwise.

Remember that the keto diet can make extreme changes in your lifestyle. If your body is used to taking in lots of carbs, then the reduction or total removal of carbs on your diet will have a significant impact on your well-being. If you are Asian and rice is a staple in your diet then you may find the keto diet to be quite challenging. The same is true for anyone who has a carb staple in their meals.

If you are experiencing seizures then your doctor might recommend that you go on a keto diet. In that case it has been deemed a good option for you. Your doctor will incorporate this mode of treatment in case seizure medications aren't working for you. Note however that your doctor or dietitian will closely monitor your progress and can call off the diet as he deems necessary.

If you have kidney issues or problems with your liver then you definitely should consult your diet first before trying the keto diet. Note that this type of diet will put more strain on these vital organs. It can even lead to fatigue and loss of muscle tissues despite the fact that you are taking in proteins.

Chapter 10: Keto Meal Plan to Boost Autophagy

In this chapter we will provide you with a sample meal plan in the ketogenic diet. This is not intended to be a comprehensive guide. There are other works that cover this topic a lot more extensively.

The goal here is to give you an idea about the meals that you can prepare, that way you can gauge whether this type of diet is for you or not. Your doctor may also prescribe this diet to you if you have any preexisting medical conditions such as the following:

- Acne
- Brain injuries
- Polycystic ovary syndrome
- Parkinson's disease
- Epilepsy (the keto diet was primarily designed for people who have epilepsy).
- Alzheimer's disease
- Cancer
- Heart disease

After going over the meal plan and the recipes, you can look for other keto recipes. You can find a lot on the web, which means you will hardly run out of options. We will also go over some tips that can be useful to you especially when you have to outside.

Foods to Avoid/Consumed Less Frequently

Note that in the keto diet any food that has high carb content shouldn't be eaten or should be consumed in minimal amounts. The following foods should either be avoided or reduced.

- *Sugar free diet foods* – yes they may say "diet" on the label but diet food and drinks are usually highly processed. On top of that, they usually contain a lot of sugar alcohol which have a huge impact on the body's ketone levels.
- *Alcohol* – alcohol usually has high carb content, which is why they aren't allowed in any keto based diet. They can literally knock you out of ketosis.
- *Unhealthy fats* – mayonnaise, processed vegetable oils, and other unhealthy fats should be limited.
- *Sauces and condiments* – be careful about sauces and condiments. Make sure that they do not contain any unhealthy fat or any form of sugar.
- *Diet products or low fat products* – diet sodas are out in this diet. Be cautious of any kind of diet- or low fat products. A lot of them are made from highly processed products and are high in carbs.
- *Tubers and root veggies* – this includes parsnips, carrots, sweet potatoes, and potatoes.
- *Legumes and beans* – this includes chickpeas, lentils, kidney beans, and peas.
- *Fruit* – all kinds of fruit intake should be reduced. Remember that a lot of fruits naturally contain sugar.

However, you can take very small portions or reduced portions of berries.
- *Starches and grains* – you should avoid eating cereal, pasta, rice, and any kind of wheat product.
- *Sugary foods* – this includes candy, ice cream, cake, smoothies, fruit juice, and of course soda.

Sample Meal Plan – Week 1

The following is the meal plan for week 1.

Monday

- Breakfast – Fried eggs with bacon
- Lunch – burger (no bread) with salsa and cheese
- Dinner – steak and eggs with a side of salad

Tuesday

- Breakfast – spinach, egg, and white fish cooked in coconut oil
- Lunch – cheese and ham slices with a side of nuts
- Dinner – cheese omelet with veggies and ham

Wednesday

- Breakfast – burger with bacon (minus the bun), cheese, and egg
- Lunch – beef stir fry with a side of veggies (use coconut oil to fry)

- Dinner – yogurt (sugar free) with stevia, cocoa powder, and peanut butter

Thursday

- Breakfast – stuffed chicken with veggies on the side. Stuffing can be cream cheese and pesto.
- Lunch – guacamole, salsa, celery sticks, and a handful of nuts
- Dinner – avocado and omelet.

Friday

- Breakfast – pork chops with salad, broccoli, and parmesan on the side
- Lunch – shrimp salad on olive oil
- Dinner – keto milkshake

Saturday

- Breakfast – meatballs with veggies and cheddar cheese
- Lunch – peanut butter, almond milk, with milkshake with stevia and cocoa powder
- Dinner – goat cheese omelet with basils and tomatoes

Sunday

- Breakfast – salmon and asparagus
- Lunch – chicken salad with feta cheese
- Dinner – eggs, bacon, and tomatoes

Sample Meal Plan – Week 2

The following is the meal plan for week 2.

Monday

- Breakfast – scrambled eggs
- Lunch – Asian beef salad
- Dinner – keto pesto chicken casserole

Tuesday

- Breakfast – keto cheese roll ups
- Lunch – keto caprese omelet
- Dinner – keto meat pie

Wednesday

- Breakfast – keto frittata with spinach on the side
- Lunch – keto chicken soup
- Dinner – keto carbonara

Thursday

- Breakfast – dairy free keto latte
- Lunch – keto salad with avocado, bacon, and goat cheese
- Dinner – keto pizza

Friday

- Breakfast – mushroom omelet
- Lunch – smoked salmon
- Dinner – keto tortilla with ground beef

Saturday

- Breakfast – baked bacon omelet
- Lunch – keto quesadillas
- Dinner – Asian cabbage stir fry

Sunday

- Breakfast – keto pancakes with whipped cream
- Lunch – Italian keto plate
- Dinner – pork chops with green beans

Keto Snacks

There are days when you will have to fast during the week. In the meal plans that you will make you should indicate which meals you will have to skip on your fasting days. You get to choose which type of intermittent fasting you will do.

In case your fasting strategy requires you to have lower calories during meals then you can use these snack ideas. They will also become useful in case you do get hungry in between meals and you really need something to eat.

You may have to break your fast at some point but at least you are still maintaining your ketosis. That way you can give your diet a bit of a push later on and still induce autophagy rather easily than not putting yourself into a keto state.

The following are keto snack ideas. However, do take note that some of these snacks may have more calories than you can imagine. It would be a good idea to do some calorie counting during your fasting days to be sure.

- Smaller portions of leftovers
- Celery with guacamole and salsa
- Strawberries with cream
- Full fat yogurt
- Low carb milkshake
- Nut butter and cocoa powder
- 90% dark chocolate
- 2 hard-boiled eggs
- Cheese and olives
- A handful of your choice of nuts or seeds
- Cheese
- Fatty fish
- Fatty meat

Eating Out/Fast Food While on a Keto Diet

This is probably one of the concerns that people who go on a diet usually have in their minds. You are on a strict and obviously different diet than most people. That means your food options are not the typical ones that you will find in your everyday menu—unless of course you're eating in a keto friendly restaurant.

Keto Friendly Restaurant Options

However, the good news is that it isn't really that hard to make regular restaurant food keto friendly. Remember that a lot of restaurants usually offer menu options that are either fish based or meat based. You can order that option and just ask to have the carb ingredients replaced with veggies.

Other than meat or fish based foods, egg meals are also another option. Omelet and bacon is a staple in low carb diet plans like keto. If you order burgers, you can ask to hold the buns and replace the fries with veggies. If you dine in a Mexican restaurant then you're in luck. You can enjoy their meat type dishes and ask for extra cheese, sour cream, salsa, and guacamole.

Keto Friendly Fast Food Options

Choosing the right fast food can be the most challenging thing to do when you're on the keto diet. Note that the keto diet is definitely a restrictive diet, which makes it kind of hard to find compatible menu options.

The hard part is in the fact that a lot of fast food options are usually high in carbs. However there are fast food chains that also serve keto friendly items on their menu. Here are several ideas on how you can make fast food keto friendly.

1. **Bunless Burgers**

The high carb levels in burger options in McDonald's, White Castle, or any other burger chain is from the buns. If you want to make these burgers keto friendly all you need to do is to get rid of the buns.

You should also ask to have some of the high carb toppings removed. Examples of these toppings are breaded onions, teriyaki sauce, ketchup, and honey mustard sauce among others.

Of course you can still have toppings on your bun-less burger. Just make sure to use keto friendly options such as tomatoes, regular onions, ranch dressing, lettuce, mustard, avocado, fried egg, salsa, and mayo.

Note that a lot of fast food stores will be happy to serve you bunless burgers if you just ask. So, how many calories will you get on the average bunless order? Here are a couple of figures that might interest you:

- Wendy's Double Stack Cheeseburger minus the bun will have 260 calories with only 20 grams protein and 1 gram of carbs
- A McDonald's Double Cheeseburger minus the bun will have 270 calories, 20 grams of protein, and 4 grams of carbs

2. Egg Breakfasts

There are many egg based breakfast options served in different fast food chains. To make them more keto friendly you can remove the hash browns, bread, and other carb sources that come with the egg. You can substitute veggies and other keto friendly options instead.

- The Burger King Ultimate Breakfast Platter minus the biscuit, hash browns, and/or pancakes gives you 340

calories total, 16 grams of protein, and only 1 gram of carbs.
- The McDonald's Bacon, Egg and Cheese Biscuit but holding the usual biscuit that is served with it gives you 190 calories, 14 grams of protein, and 4 grams of carbs.

3. Low Carb Salads

When we think of salads we think that they are usually nutrient rich foods that are low in carbs and just loaded with all the good stuff, right? Well, that is just not the case with fast food salads. A lot of them are actually loaded with carbs.

Here's an example: the Apple Pecan Chicken Salad from Wendy's sounds really safe for dieting right? But it actually has a total of 52 grams of carbs and not to mention its sugar content, which is about 40 grams per serving.

So where do all the carbs in these salads come from? They're actually found in the additives. That means you need to skip some of the usual ingredients to make them more keto friendly.

For instance you may have to remove the dried fruit, marinades, certain dressings, and toppings. Pay attention to the ingredients that are high in sugar. That means you need to avoid those sweet dressings. That means you need to stick to keto friendly dressings like ranch, vinegar, and oil.

For instance, take away all the usual carb sources from Moe's Taco Salad, you will get 325 calories, 22 grams of protein, and just 10 grams of carbs. You can keep the guacamole, cheddar cheese, jalapenos, and chicken adobo as additives. You will still be within keto bounds but you should pay attention to serving sizes.

Remember that you need to stay within the allowed number of calories to stay within a fasting zone. As it was described earlier, some fasting regimens allow around 500 to 600 calories or so per day even on a fasting day. You should avoid croutons, breaded chicken, tortilla shells, and candied nuts in order to stay within the limit of your fast.

4. Burgers in Lettuce Wraps

The good news is that fast food companies are catching on to the keto craze and they want to cash in on the rising number of customers who are opting for keto based options. That is why they are adding more keto friendly options on their menus.

An example of this is the lettuce wrapped burger. They still get to serve burgers but cutting away the majority of the carbs. Wrapping burgers in lettuce makes for a fascinating low carb option.

Here are a couple of examples:

- The Protein Style Cheeseburger from In-n-Out Burger packs around 330 calories, 18 grams of protein, and only 11 grams of carbs

- The Lettuce-Wrapped Thickburger from Carl's Jr. packs 420 calories, 25 grams of protein, and only 8 grams of carbs.

5. Low Carb Burrito Bowls

Do you know that a burrito wrap packs 50 grams of carbs which translates to 300 calories? That's just the wrapping alone—you're still not getting the entire burrito. And then comes the burrito bowl.

It's a burrito minus the wrap, basically. They have that low carb base made of leafy greens, healthy fat choices, and protein. You should avoid corn, sweet dressings, beans, and tortilla chips which are carb heavy options.

Again, you should pay attention to the calorie content and plan your meals ahead of time. Some of the burrito bowls served by popular fast food chains still have plenty of calories in them.

Here are a few examples:

- Moe's Southwestern Grill Burrito Bowl (394 calories)
- Taco Bell Cantina Power Steak Bowl (310 calories)
- Chipotle Chicken Burrito Bowl (525 calories)
- Chipotle Steak Burrito Bowl (400 calories)

If it is a fast day or you just have to cut back on your caloric intake, you can always eat half of the burrito and have the rest to go so you can keep it in the fridge for later.

6. Keto Beverage Options

It is no secret that a lot of beverages served in fast food restaurants have lots of sugar in them. Sure they call the iced tea, diet soda, sugar-free this but they are still sweet and they may have enough sugar (or sugar based substitutes) to break your ketosis.

For instance, if you order the Dunkin' Donuts Vanilla Bean Coolatta, you are still getting 88 grams of sugar. That is the equivalent of 22 teaspoons of sugar.

That is why when you order your beverages make sure that you are getting the keto friendly ones, which include the following:

- Water
- Soda water
- Hot tea (minus the sugar of course)
- Black iced coffee
- Coffee with cream
- Unsweetened iced tea

Well, what if you want to sweeten your beverage? Now what? Well, you may have to bring some zero calorie sweeteners like Stevia. Yes, it can be a bit of an inconvenience but that is a little adjustment that you will have to make if you want to maintain a ketone balance enough to induce autophagy.

Chapter 11: The Exercise-Autophagy Connection

Everyone knows that there are a lot of benefits if we engage in physical activity. The effects are of course well-known and well-researched. Well at least on the macro level. However, the cellular processes behind all those benefits have only become clearer fairly recently.

Treatment of Disorders in Skeletal Muscles

One of these relatively newer findings is the link between the prevention of the dysfunction of our muscles with exercise. One of the dysfunctions in particular that researchers are beginning to shed light on is the loss of stimuli. This frequently occurs in the skeletal muscles. Note that this is the type of muscle that makes up the most of the body's mass.

This loss of stimuli isn't because of the skeletal muscles themselves. It has more to do with the nervous system instead. The dysfunction occurs as an aftermath when the sciatic nerve gets injured.

This neural injury usually occurs on people who are bed ridden and also on people who sit for long hours such as bus drivers. Medical intervention is required in order to treat these patients and eventually improve their quality of life.

According to one study[68] from the University of São Paulo, Brazil, this type of dysfunction is due to the increased production of processed proteins in the skeletal muscles. This resulted in muscle wasting and eventual weakening of the muscular tissues.

Why was there a build-up of proteins which eventually resulted in both muscular and nerve damage? According to researchers this build up is due to the impairment of autophagy.

The loss or lack of stimulus in skeletal muscle tissues is a degenerative disease. Researchers were able to demonstrate that with exercise the skeletal muscles can be primed for autophagy. The test subjects in this study were subjected to aerobic exercises. Aerobic exercise resulted in the delay of the observed muscular atrophy.

According to Julio Cesar Batista Ferreira, daily exercise can sensitize the autophagic system. That means it doesn't only happen in the brain—it can also greatly affect the muscular tissues of the body (and perhaps other parts of the body as well).

Exercise on a daily basis facilitates the removal of dysfunctional organelles in the cells of the body—we've already touched on that several times in this book. However it should also be emphasized at this point that autophagy is also the process that eliminates unnecessary proteins that build up in the muscular tissues.

The removal of these dysfunctional components is definitely important. They are unnecessary so the body (well, the muscles in particular) don't really need them. They have no use and they have no function. But when they accumulate overtime they will become toxic. Researchers suggest that they can even contribute to muscular impairment and eventually death.

Dr. Ferreira often uses a fridge analogy to describe this kind of muscular dysfunction. He says that the muscles are like a fridge, which of course needs electricity to function. The "electricity" of course is supplied to the muscles by the sciatic nerve. Once the connection between the electricity and fridge is lost the fridge stops to function.

In the case of the muscles, the neurons stop innervating them. The food in the fridge will start to decompose or spoil. The speed of the spoilage of the food items will depend on the composition of the food. The same is true with the proteins of the muscles—they "spoil" at different rates.

How Autophagy Can Help

But Ferreira clarifies that there is a difference between a fridge and the human muscles. The muscle tissues and cells are fortunate to have an early warning system. This early warning system will activate the autophagic system at the onset of the degradation.

It isolates and "incinerates" as it were any defective material (i.e. the proteins and other toxins) that is found in the muscular tissues. This process will prevent the spread of the damage. This is basically how the autophagic system works in the muscles.

All of that is well and good. But what if autophagy is impaired? It does happen since skeletal muscles do lose stimuli. Dr. Ferreira explains that if the muscles stop receiving the right electric signals and if it continues for an extended period of time then this early warning mechanism of the muscular tissues stop to work. The result is the collapse of the cells of the skeletal muscles.

The proteins in the muscles that no longer function properly form the toxins that build up eventually. These toxins will then start killing the other cells in the muscular tissues. If autophagy is activated the process would isolate these toxic proteins and they will later be destroyed and recycled.

As you can observe from the process described above, the severed connection results in cascading effects. The end result of that series of events is the death of useful cells.

Exercise and training has been observed to increase the autophagic flux. This clean up or recycling process in the cells reduced the number of dysfunctional protein cells. At the same time exercise also improves the muscles ability to contract.

So how does that happen? Dr. Ferreira explains that exercise is a type of transient stress. This type of stress tends to create muscle memory. When human beings or any other organism is exposed or pre-exposed to certain kinds of stress it is better able to combat and respond to degenerative dysfunctions.

Dr. Ferreira's team however stresses that their research was not designed to find a solution or treatment to sciatica (i.e. the loss of stimuli to the sciatic nerve) or any other dysfunction in the muscles. They were just laying the groundwork for other research in the future.

The goal is to understand what happens to the muscles when they are subjected to exercise on the cellular level. They hope to develop a drug or a treatment regimen that may be used for patients with degenerative muscle diseases. Maybe further research can be made that may also help people with impaired limbs.

Recovery and Protection of Cardiac Muscles

Regular exercise is part of the overall treatment for heart conditions, particularly heart failure. Heart failure is a condition wherein the heart is unable to pump enough blood to supply for the entire body.

Exercise is of course beneficial to people with other related medical conditions. It is beneficial for the treatment of a variety of conditions from arterial blood pressure to cachexia (severe loss of muscle mass and weight).

We know that exercise promotes improved cardiac function. Exercise has also been found to postpone degenerative processes in heart tissues. It can help to prevent the progressive death of heart cells. Degenerative cardiac diseases are considered very serious conditions since 70% of all patients who have them tend to die from it within just 5 years.

According to one study[69] that was conducted in the University of São Paulo, Brazil, aerobic exercise has been seen to improve autophagy in the heart and protect this vital muscle. So, how does autophagy benefit heart health?

Researchers say that aerobic training increases the removal and replacement of mitochondria in the heart that are no longer functioning properly. As it was explained earlier, the mitochondria are the power house of the cells. In other words they are responsible for providing the needed energy to the cells.

When failing mitochondria is removed and eventually replaced, this improves the delivery of ATP to the cells of the heart muscle. ATP again is short for adenosine triphosphate, the molecule that stands as the energy source of the cells.

But that is not the only benefit of autophagy in the heart. When dysfunctional mitochondria are recycled the same process also reduces the production of toxic molecules in the heart. Examples of which are reactive aldehydes and oxygen free radicals, which tend to build up in the cardiac area. Excessive build-up of these toxic molecules damages the structure of the heart cells.

Putting It All Together: Exercise and Cellular Maintenance

These studies cited above confirm and reaffirm the need for exercise in the lives of people in today's modern age. Our current couch potato and sitting all day in the office culture needs to change. From the two cases—both for skeletal and cardiac muscles—we see the value of daily aerobic exercise and ability to induce autophagy.

Experts say that exercising daily will help to sensitize the body's autophagic system[70]. Exercise facilitates the removal of dysfunctional cellular components. This is important because the accumulation of these dysfunctional components whether they be mitochondria, proteins, or others will cause a toxic build up and eventual degeneration and impairment of nearby muscular tissues. The final effect of this toxic build up is cellular death.

Aerobic vs. Anaerobic Exercise

In the studies that we highlighted, the researchers used aerobic exercise as the primary exercise regimen to induce autophagy. Now the question here is that do just do aerobic exercises or can we do anaerobic exercises as well?

Well, before any of that we should first identify the difference between aerobic and anaerobic exercises. To put it all simply, aerobic exercises constitutes any light activity. If it is an exercise that you can do and sustain for a long period of time then that is considered as an aerobic exercise.

Examples of these exercises include jogging, walking, swimming, and cycling. These are exercises that you can keep doing for hours on end without getting absolutely fatigued. That is not the case with anaerobic exercises.

Anaerobic exercises are the types of activities that will leave you running out of breath within a few minutes. They are more of bust exercises that can only be done for a very short span of time. Examples of these exercises include sprinting and weight lifting.

During aerobic exercises you are able to supply oxygen to the body since you have enough power left to inhale and exhale while performing the said exercise. That is not the case with anaerobic exercise. In that mode the activity that you are doing is so difficult and your actions so vigorous that you hardly have enough time or energy to breath. You will be forced to stop exercising just to be able to breathe.

So, which one is better?

The truth is that both types of exercise burns fat. Both of them will give your metabolism a boost. And that caloric burn will go on for a few hours even after you have worked out. That means in order to give the biggest boost to your autophagic system you should incorporate both exercises when you work out.

Aerobic exercises increase muscular endurance. It also improves your cardiac health. Anaerobic exercises help you burn more body fat and also helps you gain lean muscle mass, which is important to prevent muscular atrophy (aka muscle loss).

Aerobic and Anaerobic Exercise Samples

You don't necessarily have to go to the gym to exercise. You can do it all in th comforts of your own home. The following are examples of aerobic exercises that you can try:

- Ride a stationary bike
- Go bicycling around the block
- Play tennis
- Play badminton
- Ice skating
- Roller skating
- Swimming
- Dancing
- Follow an aerobic workout on TV or YouTube
- Jogging
- Run or jog on a treadmill
- Jog every morning or afternoon
- Jumping jacks
- Brisk walk around the neighborhood

The following are examples of anaerobic exercises that you can do at home. Note that you can purchase weights if you want or just find heavy objects that you can safely lift. Another option is to do bodyweight exercises (i.e. calisthenics).

- Sprints (you can do 2 minutes of running as fast as you can, rest for 1 minute, and run at a moderate pace for another minute, then rest for another minute and then repeat from the start).
- Weight lifting (again you can use weights but you can also just use objects that are sufficiently heavy like bottled water, a backpack full of books, etc.)
- Calisthenics like inclined pushups, pushups, sit ups, chin-ups, bench dips, and knee raises
- Plyometric exercises like jump rope, lunges, skipping, clap push-ups, and jump squats (note that some of these exercises can be intense for someone who hasn't done any exercise for a long time). I suggest that you reserve these exercises for later.
- Isometric exercises like forearm planks, low squats, triceps extension against the wall, prayer pose, high planks, bent over presses against the wall.

Tips for People Who Haven't Exercised in a Long Time

If you haven't done any cardio exercises in a while then you shouldn't go gung ho about it. Start slowly. You don't want to put undue strain on your limbs, which will take the brunt of the punishment.

Do things gradually and start out with just a short 5 to 10 minute workout (maybe brisk walking first?) each day for a week. Allow your feet, legs, and lungs to slowly regain their strength. Basically what you're doing is acclimating your body to workouts and exercises.

If 5 to 10 minutes of cardio every day seems too much then start with cardio 2 to 3 times a week. Do your cardio for 2 weeks or until your body has become used to walking or jogging.

The following week you can take things up a notch. You can either try a more intensive workout or just increase the time you exercise. Let's say you just used to walk on two separate days each week for 10 minutes, you can try walking 15 minutes every day next week.

Another option is to go jogging for 10 minutes on two separate days in the next week. The following week you can try jogging 5 minutes every day. And then the following week you can go jogging for 15 minutes every day in the morning or afternoon.

After that you can try running instead. But you should reduce your workout time so as not to strain your joints especially your knees. You can also switch to swimming or dancing which is more intense. You should do things progressively.

If you miss a day of workouts or if you are sore then you can of course take the day off and rest for a day or two. Give your body time to recover. Don't push yourself too much. What you want to happen is to incorporate exercise into your daily routine along with the other practices that we have covered in this book such as fasting and a keto diet. The end goal of course is to induce autophagy.

Should I Do HIIT?

HIIT or high intensity interval training transforms your usual cardio exercise into a very powerful aerobic exercise. Should you do HIIT? It depends on your fitness level and your diet.

Yes you will get the most of your workout time by doing HIIT but note that this type of training is really intense. It is one of the most demanding forms of training out there. If you are on the keto diet or any low carb diet then doing HIIT is a recipe for disaster.

If you plan on doing HIIT then you should be done with your low carb diet. That means you're back to the regular carb levels. If you haven't had a sandwich (not the keto approved breadless sandwich kind) then HIIT is not for you.

You should do this type of training after you have established that you can get back to fasting and low carb diet. If you're looking for workouts just to stimulate autophagy then HIIT is not for you. It may possibly end up in muscle loss or you may not be able to finish the training anyway.

What About High Altitude Training?

High altitude training is another controversial kind of workout. Yes, high altitude training is able to improve the function of skeletal muscles. However, there isn't sufficient evidence that this type of training regimen can positively impact or contribute to autophagy. In fact, you can also get the same autophagic stimulation if you do cardio for 2 to 7 days straight. Until further evidence can be cited in favor of high altitude training, we can't recommend it as a method to induce autophagy—in short we're on a wait and see mode for now.

Chapter 12: Deep Sleep and Autophagy

One of the simplest things that you can do to help induce autophagy is to get some quality sleep. There is a link between autophagy and the body's circadian rhythm. The circadian rhythm is the sleep-wake cycle that we all go through.

It's a Matter of Cycles

As a matter of fact, a lot of things in this life and not just sleep and wakefulness have cyclic patterns. That also includes living and dying both on the macro and micro levels of life. Cycles are present not only in the body but also in our environment.

Circadian rhythms are more than just sleeping at night and waking up in the morning. There are a lot of physiological processes that go on behind the scenes while you are awake and while you sleep. These same processes govern the circadian rhythm as well as the body's autophagic systems.

And guess what—autophagy is a re-"cycling" process. Old cellular parts are cycled over to be reused. In that process there is also a clean-up that happens and waste is dumped out of the body's systems. It is again a cycle – in this case on the cellular level.

Autophagy itself is part of another cycle—one of feeding and not feeding. Coincidentally we feed usually when we are awake, unless you can go sleep eating of course but that's a different matter altogether. A lot of the info we have about the molecular systems involved that control the circadian rhythm come from the works of Nobel Prize winning physiologists Michael W. Young, Michael Rosbash, and Jeffrey C. Hall.

Sleep and Autophagy

Getting quality sleep is a crucial factor if you want to get the best benefits from autophagy. Melatonin is called the sleep hormone and it has been found to modulate the body's autophagic processes[71]. It is also a very powerful antioxidant.

It also controls a lot of the other repairs that go on in the body as you sleep. On top of that it also controls the release of the body's growth hormone. That is how vital this hormone is to the human body.

The growth hormone is also just as important as melatonin. Studies have shown that 70% of growth hormone pulses that we experience each day only happen during deep sleep[72]. It facilitates fat burning, regeneration, and other physical repairs. It also acts on the liver to stimulate or induce the autophagic process.

Again, remember that the growth hormone is stimulated by melatonin. That is why your body should be able to produce sufficient amounts of that hormone. How does your body produce it? Melatonin is produced only in the absence of green and blue light—it only occurs in darkness.

If you want to increase the autophagic processes in the body then you should optimize your sleep in order to increase melatonin production. You need to get enough sleep at night. That means you should get enough sleep time and you should also sleep at the right time.

It should also be noted that both AMPK and mTOR (the two pathways for autophagy and growth respectively) are also regulated by melatonin[73]. Remember that as it was described in previous chapters that AMPK promotes autophagy, cell breakdown, catabolism, and also ketosis. mTOR on the other hand promotes nerve proliferation, bone enhancement, protein synthesis, as well as cellular growth.

AMPK can be activated using calorie restriction, low carb diets, fasting, and exercise. mTOR on the other hand is activated by excess calories, increased insulin levels in the blood, eating lots of carbs, consuming protein, and resistance training.

Circadian Rhythms and Autophagy

It should also be pointed out that even the autophagic process has a diurnal rhythm as well. It can be observed occurring in the muscles, heart, and also the liver[74]. We know that fasting creates conditions that are optimal for the kick starting of autophagy.

However, an equally important thing to consider is the timing. When does autophagy usually take place? Studies show that autophagy gets activated usually during times of low metabolic activity—i.e. when your body isn't busy doing other stuff.

That usually happens during fasting—since you are not eating and there is no food that your digestive system is working on. It also occurs during times of caloric restriction (i.e. when you eat less food). It also happens when you experience energy stress (i.e. when you are exercising). And now we know that autophagy is also activated when we sleep.

Remember that when you are awake and the body is busy doing all the other processes dictated by your metabolism, then there is no time for it to perform any repairs. The body is said to be in its growth state at such times. But when it shuts down the growth phase (or an active phase) and moves on to other things, the body focuses on repair as well as in self-healing.

Quality sleep is an essential if you want to achieve autophagy. Even though you put in some time to fast short term or long term and you do regular exercises, it might not be enough to stimulate autophagy if you do not allow your body to enter into repair mode—that is why you need to put in some time to sleep (which should be around 7 to 10 hours at night).

That means everything that you do to prep your body to enter into autophagy gets stacked up as it were. They get installed and wait for something to happen before their benefits can be reaped. You finally get to reap those benefits when melatonin is produced in your brain—and then the work of autophagic processes rolls forward. In this essence getting quality sleep is essential to an overall plan if you want to induce natural self-healing.

How to Support Melatonin Production

Since melatonin production is critical to autophagy you should know how to help your brain produce more of this hormone. Here are a few tips that may help you get better sleep, improve melatonin production, and help you get a better circadian rhythm.

- When you wake up in the morning make sure that you expose your eyes to sunlight. This sets up your circadian rhythm.
- Turn off cellphones and even your home's WIFI. You should also shut down any other electrical devices in your room. What you want to achieve is the reduced exposure to EMF, which negatively impacts melatonin secretion.
- Avoid drinking any kind of alcoholic drink before going to bed
- Reduce stress (this can be a bit challenging for some people).
- Sleep in a dark environment. That means close the curtains and/or wear a sleep mask

- Avoid caffeine in the afternoon or in the evening
- Don't watch any scary, action packed, or otherwise stimulating movie or video before going to bed.
- Don't eat anything 3 hours before going to bed.
- Turn off sources of blue light at night—switch to non-blue light emitting bulbs at night.
- Maintain a regular sleeping schedule

Chapter 13: Time Restricted Feeding

What is Time Restricted Feeding?

According research all living organisms have a consolidated time for actively being awake and also sleeping. During this cycle they also go through a time for sleeping and repair/healing. This is the phase for inactivity and as it was explained earlier the healing is booted when you go fasting. We have a feeding plus awake phase of the cycle and a sleep plus fasting cycle.

And here is where the concept of Time Restricted Feeding (TRF) comes in. What is TRF? Simply put it means that you will eat food within a given time frame. This time frame should coincide with the body's circadian rhythm. Researchers say that the act of eating the calories that we consume has a huge impact on the brain's SCN or suprachiasmatic nucleus[75]. The SCN is the master clock inside of us.

Studies indicate that human beings usually have a 15 hour feeding period. Roughly 13 hours of that is done when we are awake during the day time and the last 2 hours are done during the night at dinner time, usually. Experts recommend that people should only eat within an 8 to 10 hour feeding period if you don't want your caloric intake to interfere with your circadian rhythm.

Whenever we fast—whether it is at night when we sleep or any time when we are awake—both the immune system and the digestive system are given time to make needed repairs and let the processes of autophagy do their thing[76].

TRF vs. Intermittent Fasting

Some people believe that there is a difference between TRF and intermittent fasting. The truth of the matter is that sometimes both of these terms are used interchangeably. So when you read text about them you should consider the context. But there are a few subtle differences.

We can also say that intermittent fasting is the blanket term that people use to describe any practice that involves the suppression of eating on a recurring basis. And TRF is a type of intermittent fasting—it can be considered as part of that blanket term or category.

But there are differences—so let's go over those a little bit. Intermittent fasting is more concerned about going through a cycle of eating followed by a period of not eating. An example of this is the alternate day fast where you fast in one day but then you have regular meals the following day. Extended fasting can also be seen as cyclic in a way since you will not eat for several days and then eat again in the next following days.

TRF on the other hand can also be considered as a form of fasting because you do not eat after a given time. On top of that you also follow a cyclic period. The big emphasis in time restricted feeding however is that you can only eat within a specified time frame. For instance, if you follow an 6/18 window then that would mean that you are only allowed to eat within 6 hours a day and you should not eat anything the rest of the day.

2 Types of TRF

There are actually two types of time restricted feeding (or time restricted eating). The first one is called Early TRF and the other one is Late TRF. Early TRF means that you will eat usually in the morning and stop sometime after lunch.

An example of early TRF would be having breakfast at 8 am and maybe having a snack before lunch. And then you can have your lunch at noon. And then after that perhaps one last snack at 2 pm could be placed in your schedule. After 2 pm no more eating will be allowed.

Late TRF on the other hand would mean that you are only allowed to eat during the later parts of the day. You are going to skip breakfast and you will schedule your lunch at a later time—not at noon. Let's say that your eating window starts at 2 pm, that is the only time when you will have lunch. You can schedule other meals until 10 pm. No more meals can be had after 10 pm.

Given the description of TRF, anyone who does the Warrior Diet, the 16/8 diet, or even the OMAD (one meal a day) are technically doing a type of intermittent fasting called TRF.

Benefits of Time Restricted Feeding

TRF does not necessarily reduce one's calorie intake. Yet studies have shown that it can prevent metabolic syndrome as well as obesity. Studies also suggest that it can also prevent the development of heart disease. Those who undergo TRF also experience improvement in glucose control[77].

The same research pointed out that eating the same amount of food within a window of 6 hours in TRF can improve one's blood pressure, insulin sensitivity, and glycemic control. This showed better results than people who ate food when they were given a 12 hour window for eating (i.e. they were allowed to eat for 12 hours instead of just 6 hours).

In that same review the effect of TRF was compared to men who were weight training. Both groups basically were doing resistance training. One group was given only a 12 hour eating period where they should eat their meals. After that no more meals were served. The other group followed the 16/8 fasting regimen as it was described in a previous chapter of this book.

The results showed that both groups had the same improvements when it came to muscle growth and strength (yes, you can still workout in the gym even if you are on a fasting regimen). But the group that went through the 16/8 method had better results when it came to fat burning. That meant that their autophagic systems were running well given their schedule.

These studies exemplify the great benefits of TRF. These benefits actually come from the fact that time restricted feeding is better at suppressing insulin. It also allows you to stay in a fasted state much longer. It also better allows the body to enter into a state of autophagy.

Early TRF or Late TRF: Which One is Better?

The next question that people ask is if Early TRF is better than Late TRF. There was one study that tried that[78] and here are their findings. The study involved 15 men who were already diagnosed as obese. They were required to go through TRF with a 9 hour eating window and they started with Early TRF.

They did that for a week having breakfast at 8 am and their last meal for the day at 5 pm. They ate normally, which meant that they did not binge eat or anything—just the same balanced diet. That also meant that they never went hungry at any time during the day.

After a week their stats were taken and then the test subjects changed their eating schedule. This time they went on Late TRF the following week. After that they ate normally to negate any adaptations that their bodies have undergone.

What they found out was that it doesn't matter whether you did Late TRF or Early TRF. You still get the same benefits from time restricted feeding. The men who went through both regimens practically reaped the same benefits—that is if you take only the glycemic control, insulin levels, energy expenditure, and other related results into consideration.

Adding Melatonin Production into the Equation

The big difference between Early TRF and Late TRF happens when you add melatonin production into the factors that you should consider. Remember that the pancreas tends to produce more insulin during the day than at night. That means blood sugar happens much better during the day time than at night[79].

The melatonin production levels in the body usually begin a few hours before the usual time you go to bed. The only thing that will stop this production is when you are exposed to a lot of blue or green light as it was explained in chapter 12 previously.

When melatonin levels increase they can bind better to their receptors that can be found in the pancreas. Now, we don't need to get too technical on that but that simply means the melatonin is signaling or telling the pancreas to stop the production of insulin. In other words this hormone is signaling your pancreas that bed time is almost near and your body doesn't need to process any more energy[80].

That is how it should work normally but there are things that can disrupt this pattern. One of those things is eating a big meal before going to bed—especially one that is high in carbs. If that is the case and the pancreas stops producing insulin, then there will not be enough insulin left in your blood stream to process the remaining glucose.

That will result in a strained system and you may not be able to sleep that well for the night. The quality of your sleep will be affected and thus autophagy may be impaired for that night.

But there is a huge BUT that we can throw into that mix.

You see, eating a huge meal at night and lowered insulin production may only affect you if you go on short term fasts. If you are already on a long term extended fast your insulin sensitivity may already be very high.

That means even if you ate a huge meal in the evening and you are still highly insulin sensitive then your body can still process the remaining glucose even if the pancreas has already reduced its insulin production.

Nevertheless, the big issue here is that if eating at night (or fasting at night) will disrupt your melatonin production then you should opt for Early TRF or some other fasting routine that won't make you eat at night.

Chapter 14: Heat Exposure

One of the methods to induce autophagy that was mentioned earlier in chapter 3 of this book is hot and cold exposure. This type of changing exposures creates cellular stress and this is the factor initiates or at least contributes to autophagy. In this chapter we will go over the possible use of saunas and heat shock response. In the next chapter we will cover cryotherapy and other hot and cold methods and how they may help to stimulate cellular repair in the body.

Saunas and Heat Shock Response

There are several medical studies that have tackled the subject of heat shock response and heat stress and how they can stimulate autophagy. According to one study autophagy and apoptosis can be induced due to heat stress. Several studies suggest that heat shock proteins are formed when the body is exposed to heat and these proteins are involved in the maintenance of healthy cells and of course autophagy[81].

Knowing that kind of gives you a hint that there is something about saunas that can be beneficial to one's health. In fact saunas or some other form of heat therapy are part of many cultures in the world. Heat therapy has long been recognized as therapeutic even before the modern medical world has noticed its benefits. Many people have been dipping in hot pools, taking hot baths, and enjoying saunas for thousands of years.

Today we have a lot of scientific studies that support the health benefits of heat therapy and its effects on human longevity. A sauna is basically just a heated room—some people call them sweat lodges.

Here are some of the benefits of heat exposure via saunas, sweat lodges, hot baths etc.

- According to one study, it is suggested that taking sauna baths around 4 to 7 times a week can reduce one's mortality rate by 40% [82].
- Heat exposure that produces heat shock response has been found to increase brain neurotrophic factors and also raise the brain's endorphin levels.
- Taking sauna baths have been linked to a lowered risk for Alzheimer's and dementia[83].
- Maintains a youthful appearance by clearing the skin
- Flushes the lymphatic system of pathogens and other toxins
- Increases the number of white blood cells and strengthens the immune system
- Improves the strove volume of the heart to increase one's physical endurance (*Thermoregulatory Responses to Acute Exercise-Heat Stress and Heat Acclimation. Kent B. Pandolf, Michael N. Sawka, C. B. W. Handbook of Physiology, Environmental Physiology, 2011.*)

- Improves blood flow to skeletal muscles and increases overall blood circulation
- Lowers the heart rate and improves overall cardiovascular health (*Hannuksela, M. L. & Ellahham, S. Benefits and risks of sauna bathing. The American journal of medicine 110, 118-126, 2001*)

In many cultures saunas and hot baths have other uses other than just for bathing, self-washing, and getting clean. In some cultures mothers give birth in saunas. In others, they wash their dead in saunas as part of the ritual in burial preparation. In many instances, the sauna or hot room is usually the cleanest part of the house.

The Production of Heat Shot Proteins

We mentioned heat shock proteins (or HSPs) as part of the benefits that are produced when you go through heat therapy (e.g. taking a sauna bath). But what are heat shock proteins?

HSPs refer to an entire family of proteins that are produced by the body when it experiences heat stress. It is one of the ways the body responds to experiencing heat—in other words the body produces HSPs to adapt to increased temperature. The body releases HSPs due to environmental conditions that give rise to water deprivation, hypoxia, starvation, heat stress, and inflammation[84].

HSPs actually have a number of health benefits, which include the following:

- Studies suggest that HSPs may be able to increase one's lifespan by at least 15% (*Khazaeli, A. A., Tatar, M., Pletcher, S. D. & Curtsinger, J. W. Heat-induced longevity extension in Drosophila. I. Heat treatment, mortality, and thermotolerance. The journals of gerontology. Series A, Biological sciences and medical sciences 52, B48-52, 1997*)
- HSPs have been found to be involved in cellular turnover and also macroautophagy
- They help promote the body's antioxidant capacity
- They prevent cell damage and the accumulation of free radicals
- They also promote the repair of misfolded proteins which is the same action that occurs during autophagy (*Naito, H. et al. Heat stress attenuates skeletal muscle atrophy in hindlimb-unweighted rats. J Appl Physiol 88, 359-363, 2000*).

The research suggests that there are plenty of benefits that can be gained from heat shock proteins as they are mediated by autophagy. However, some may ask if heat exposure can actually damage cells and eventually lead to cell death.

That is indeed a valid concern and it is also a natural phenomenon. If there is indeed too much heat then the cells will eventually die. But the body has a natural protective mechanism against heat stress on the cellular level—mitochondrial autophagy. This protective metabolic state turns on when the body experiences heat shock that can induce the death of cells (i.e. apoptosis).

This is one of the body's adaptations to environmental stress[85]. However, if the body's autophagic system is blocked or impaired then exposure to heat stress via saunas or other similar treatments may not be as beneficial as it should be.

Heat Stress Encourages Growth Hormone Release

In reality exposure to any kind of stressor from the environment has the potential to make the body stronger. This might remind you of the adage that what doesn't kill you only makes you stronger—it is very real in this case. Examples of environmental stressors can include exercise, fasting, calorie restriction, cold temperatures, and of course heat exposure. These things can make you healthier and also stronger through experience and adaptation.

Heat stress also aids in the release of the body's growth hormone. This growth hormone as it was described in previous chapters helps to inhibit protein breakdown. The growth hormone doesn't help you build muscle or anything instead it helps to prevent muscular catabolism.

When something is in a catabolic state or is in catabolism it breaks down its complex components into smaller ones. It is the opposite of anabolism, which refers to the build-up of something—in this case muscular anabolism refers to the building of muscles whereas muscular catabolism is its opposite. The growth hormone helps protect your muscles from breakdown during stressful conditions.

Combine that with fasting and you will see a growth hormone production boost of up to 2000%[86]. The catch of course is that you should stay fasted for at least 24 hours if you want to achieve that level of catabolism in the body.

That means it will be a pretty good idea to take sauna baths or at least a hot bath when you are fasting. Not only will this practice help you promote additional fat burning effects but it will also induce anti-catabolic effects. In other words, it helps boost the autophagic systems of the body.

Sauna Baths to Induce Autophagy

How do you take a sauna so that you can induce autophagy? There are a few factors to consider when answering this question. How long do you have to spend in a sauna? What is the optimal temperature that you have to set? How many times do you have to go into the sauna to get the desired effects? Can you do it every day?

Research shows that people should go into saunas and stay there for 15 to 30 minutes to get the most benefits from it. The temperature for each sauna session should be anywhere from 156°F to 212°F or 70°C to 100°C.

Experts recommend that people do saunas around 2 up to 4 times a week. Do take note that doing more saunas will not translate to reaping more health benefits. You see it's going to be like that crab in hot water phenomenon. You put a crab in a pot and slowly raise the temperature ever so slowly.

The crab won't notice the subtle increase in temperature. It slowly acclimates to the warm environment. And before long it is cooking in its own bath as it were. The same is true for human beings, unfortunately.

If you have too many frequent saunas your body will get used to the heat, which means you will have to increase the temperature to induce hormesis (i.e. the point where your body reacts to the heat and trigger that adaptive healing response). That simply means it isn't a good idea to do saunas every day.

Supporting Medical Studies

There are medical studies that suggest that heat exposure via saunas promote longevity in the human body similar to the effects of intermittent fasting. There was a study in conducted in Finland where one group of test subjects had saunas 2 to 3 times each week and another group had saunas only once a week.

The results suggest that those who had more frequent saunas had reduced their chances of dying via cardiac related conditions down to 22%, which is much lower compared to the group that only had one sauna session per week. It was also suggested that the more frequent you go to the sauna increases your survivability from cardiovascular disease by 50% to 63%.

Infrared Sauna Autophagy

The sauna sessions that we have been describing thus far have been those of traditional saunas where steam and other usual heating methods are used. These are the saunas that can reach temperatures of 70-100°C.

There are other types of saunas. Well they are more modern versions of the traditional sauna known as infrared saunas. These modern saunas heat the body directly unlike the traditional ones that heat the air surrounding the body. They generally have a higher heat range anywhere from 120 °F to 140 °F or 50 °C to 60 °C.

Now, even though they have a different mode of action when it comes to heating they also provide you with the same health benefits. They can also help reduce inflammation, improve blood circulation, promote better sleep, and induce relaxation.

Regular saunas on the other hand can stimulate lymph flow and open the skin's pores—something that infrared saunas can't mimic. However, infrared saunas have their unique set of benefits such as deeply penetrating into the body's organs, muscles, and joints.

The big downside to using infrared saunas is the fact that they emit electromagnetic radiation (EMF). That is why if you are in the market for an infrared sauna unit or before you step into one, you should check whether or not it is low EMF type.

Safety Rules for Using Saunas

Over exposure to heat can be dangerous no matter how much autophagy it can stimulate. If you have preexisting medical conditions then a sauna may not be a good idea. Make sure to check with your doctor before proceeding with it.

Here are a few safety precautions and rules to help you stay safe when you take a sauna.

1. Don't stay in a sauna for too long. If it is your first time and you aren't accustomed to the heat then shorten your stay to a few minutes. On average your max time per session should be around 15 to 20 minutes. The most that you can stay is 30 minutes but never longer. Note that the length of time the body can tolerate the heat in a sauna will vary from one person to the next.
2. Remember to rehydrate after a sauna session. You may also want to eat something a bit salty since salt enhances water retention in the body.
3. Rest for at least 10 minutes after your session. Give your body time to recuperate. This is the period when your body is stimulated to heal itself.
4. Never go alone as much as possible. Some people may pass out due to the heat and you don't want to be alone in such circumstances. You can't always count on the staff of a spa to come rescue you. There is a good reason why saunas are shared with other folks.

5. Take the time to cool down—you may even want to take a cold bath after, which follows a tradition in Finland. Well, they jump into the snow after a sauna but you can take less extreme means to cool down like maybe a cold bath. Doing so may help to prevent the reabsorption of the impurities that your body has just eliminated via the heat exposure.
6. Never drink alcohol while having a sauna. The National Stroke Association has correlated taking alcohol during a sauna to cause stroke and possible death.
7. Don't have a large meal after a sauna session
8. Leave the sauna immediately if you feel dizzy, nauseous, or you feel a headache coming on.
9. Don't bring your cellphone with you in the sauna
10. Don't have a sauna if you are pregnant
11. Don't go into the sauna naked—some people do but you shouldn't do it. It's unsanitary.
12. Don't wear any jewelry. Don't even wear your watch—remember that metal heats up quickly. There is usually a timer in there.

Chapter 15: Hot and Cold Therapy

One of the safety tips mentioned in the previous chapter mentioned a Finnish tradition where people jump into icy cold water or the snow right after a sauna. This hot and cold exposure is believed by researchers to promote neural autophagy[87]. These studies of course are in their initial stages but there is reason to believe that there is a strong correlation between hot and cold exposure to inducing autophagy, though indirectly.

This has something to do with the production of cold shock proteins (CSPs) in the human body. Just like HSPs, cold shock proteins are produced by the body as an adaptive and protective response but this time as an adaptation to cold temperatures.

CSPs and Their Benefits

Cold shock proteins are one of the most reserved proteins in the body. They are reserved for special circumstances—when you are exposed to extreme cold. Note that CSPs are also present in other organisms especially the ones that hibernate during the winter.

Note however that the term CSD is a blanket term that is used to refer to an entire family of proteins that are produced in response to cold temperature. Some CSDs are particularly targeted for cancer therapy like the Y-box protein-1 [88].

As you may have already guessed there are benefits that can be gained from the induction of CSPs in the body—and they can also help to induce autophagy. Here are some of their benefits:

- Winter swimming has been observed to reduce uric acid levels in the body[89].
- Cold exposure activates the body's brown adipose tissue which can improve the function of the mitochondria in cells[90].
- Increasing CSPs in the body coincides with the increased production of adiponectin, which can help regulate insulin in the blood[91].
- Cold exposure also increases the production of norepinephrine, which can reduce inflammation and provide other health benefits[92].

Do CSPs and Cold Exposure Induce Autophagy?

The short and sweet answer to the question above is no—cold exposure does not *directly* influence autophagy in the cells. However, heat shock does[93] induce autophagy. What happens is that cold exposure indirectly influences this metabolic state. It follows a different pathway to help induce it.

Combining cold showers or ice baths after a sauna can boost the health benefits that you can gain from HSPs. You can also do it the other way around. You can take a mildly cold shower and then go rewarm yourself through either a hot bath or a sauna. This cold to heat process encourages the production of the LC3 protein, which is known to promote autophagy[94].

How to Safely Do Hot and Cold Therapy

You should take care when you do hot and cold therapy just as you would take precautions before do a sauna. For starters, you can sit in a sauna for 5 to 10 minutes. Make sure to follow the safety rules mentioned in the previous chapter.

You should have an ice bath prepared beforehand. This can be made of a tub with water and ice. The ice bath doesn't need to be freezing cold. It should at least be cold enough so that you can tolerate the cooler temperature. After your sauna you can take a dip in the ice bath for 2 minutes and then dry off.

Another way to do it is to sauna for 5 minutes followed by a cold shower for 2 minutes and then back into the sauna again for another 10 minutes. After that you cool off and hydrate.

Conclusion

I'd like to thank you and congratulate you for transiting my lines from start to finish.

I hope this book was able to help you to understand what autophagy is and how you can enhance it. Remember that there is still a lot of ongoing research about this subject. We may not have yet been able to produce a pill or a treatment protocol that can induce or enhance autophagy. But the strategies mentioned here in this book can help prime your body so that it can enter into a state of autophagy for increased healing and wellness.

Thanks for reading, and I wish you the best of luck.

Mark Evans

Thank you

Before you go, I just wanted to say thank you for purchasing my book.

You could have picked from dozens of other books on the same topic but you took a chance and chose this one.

So, a HUGE thanks to you for getting this book and for reading all the way to the end.

Now I wanted to ask you for a small favor. ***Could you please consider posting a review on the platform? Reviews are one of the easiest ways to support the work of authors.***

This feedback will help me continue to write the type of books that will help you get the results you want. So if you enjoyed it, please let me know.

Resource Page/Sources Cited

1. White, Eileen and DiPaola, Robert S. (2009 August 25). The Double-edged Sword of Autophagy Modulation in Cancer. Retrieved from https://www.ncbi.nlm.nih.gov/pmc/articles/PMC2737083/

2. Altman BJ and Rathmell JC (2009 May). Autophagy: not good OR bad, but good AND bad. Retrieved from https://www.ncbi.nlm.nih.gov/pubmed/19398886

3. Amaravadi, Ravi, Kimmelman, Alec C., and White, Eileen. (2016 September 1). Recent insights into the function of autophagy in cancer. Retrieved from https://www.ncbi.nlm.nih.gov/pmc/articles/PMC5066235/

4. Kim I, Lemasters JJ. (2010 November 24). Mitochondrial degradation by autophagy (mitophagy) in GFP-LC3 transgenic hepatocytes during nutrient deprivation. Retrieved from https://www.ncbi.nlm.nih.gov/pubmed/21106691

5. Pietrocola F, Pol J, Vacchelli E, Rao S, Enot DP. (2016 July 11). Caloric Restriction Mimetics Enhance Anticancer Immunosurveillance. Retrieved from https://www.ncbi.nlm.nih.gov/pubmed/27411589.

6. Alirezaei et. al. (2010 August 6). Short-term fasting induces profound neuronal autophagy. Retrieved from https://www.ncbi.nlm.nih.gov/pubmed/20534972.

7. Alirezaei et. al. (2010 August 14). Short-term fasting induces profound neuronal autophagy. Retrieved from https://www.ncbi.nlm.nih.gov/pmc/articles/PMC3106288/

8. Alirezaei, Mehrdad et. al. (2010 August 16). Short-term fasting induces profound neuronal autophagy. Retrieved from https://www.tandfonline.com/doi/full/10.4161/auto.6.6.12376.

9. He, Congcong, Sumpter, Rhea Jr., Levine, Beth. (2012 October 1). Exercise induces autophagy in peripheral tissues and in the brain. Retrieved from https://www.ncbi.nlm.nih.gov/pmc/articles/PMC3463459/

10. He C, Sumpter R Jr, Levine B. (2012 October 8). Exercise induces autophagy in peripheral tissues and in the brain. Retrieved from https://www.ncbi.nlm.nih.gov/pubmed/22892563.

11. Congcong He, Sumpter Rhea Jr., Levine Beth. (2012 August 15). Exercise induces autophagy in peripheral tissues and in the brain. Retrieved from https://www.tandfonline.com/doi/full/10.4161/auto.21327#.Vdyc87J3nIU

12. McCarty MF, DiNicolantonio JJ, O'Keefe JH. (2015 November). Ketosis may promote brain macroautophagy by activating Sirt1 and hypoxia-inducible factor-1. Retrieved from https://www.ncbi.nlm.nih.gov/pubmed/26306884

13. Funderburk, Sarah F. PhD, Marcellino, Bridget K. BA, and Yue, Zhenyu PhD (2010 January). Cell "Self-Eating"

(Autophagy) Mechanism in Alzheimer's Disease. Retrieved from https://www.ncbi.nlm.nih.gov/pmc/articles/PMC2835623/

14. Wang BH et. al. (2018 January 1) Ketogenic diet attenuates neuronal injury via autophagy and mitochondrial pathways in pentylenetetrazol-kindled seizures. Retrieved from https://www.ncbi.nlm.nih.gov/pubmed/29056525

15. Zhang M, Jiang M, Bi Y, Zhu H, Zhou Z, Sha J. (2012 July 25). Autophagy and Apoptosis Act as Partners to Induce Germ Cell Death after Heat Stress in Mice. Retrieved from http://journals.plos.org/plosone/article?id=10.1371/journal.pone.0041412.

16. Neutelings Thibaut, Lambert Charles A., Nusgens Betty V., and Colige Alain C. (2013 July 23). Effects of Mild Cold Shock (25°C) Followed by Warming Up at 37°C on the Cellular Stress Response. Retrieved from https://journals.plos.org/plosone/article?id=10.1371/journal.pone.0069687

17. He Y et. al. (2016 April 14). Circadian rhythm of autophagy proteins in hippocampus is blunted by sleep fragmentation. Retrieved from https://www.ncbi.nlm.nih.gov/pubmed/27078501.

18. Qiu H, Li S, Le W. (2015 July). Impacts of chronic sleep deprivation on learning and memory, autophagy and neuronal apoptosis in mice. Retrieved from https://www.researchgate.net/publication/282903173_Imp

acts_of_chronic_sleep_deprivation_on_learning_and_memory_autophagy_and_neuronal_apoptosis_in_mice.

19. Ma, S Li, Molusky, and J Lin. (2012 April 18). Circadian autophagy rhythm: a link between clock and metabolism? Retrieved from https://www.ncbi.nlm.nih.gov/pmc/articles/PMC3389582/

20. Mahmood et. al. (2016 September). Advancing role of melatonin in the treatment of neuropsychiatric disorders. Retrieved from https://www.sciencedirect.com/science/article/pii/S231480 8X16300197

21. Zhou et. al. (2011 August 25). Melatonin protects against rotenone-induced cell injury via inhibition of Omi and Bax-mediated autophagy in Hela cells. Retrieved from https://www.ncbi.nlm.nih.gov/pubmed/21883444

22. Luo, Chen, Liang. (2017 November 27). Modulation of Acupuncture on Cell Apoptosis and Autophagy. Retrieved from https://www.hindawi.com/journals/ecam/2017/8268736/

23. Tian et. al. (2016 January 21). Acupuncture promotes mTOR-independent autophagic clearance of aggregation-prone proteins in mouse brain. Retrieved from https://www.nature.com/articles/srep19714

24. Liu et. al. (2017 April 7). Neuroprotection of hyperbaric oxygen treatment for traumatic brain injury involving autophagy pathway in rats. Retrieved from https://www.dovepress.com/neuroprotection-of-

hyperbaric-oxygen-treatment-for-traumatic-brain-inj-peer-reviewed-article-JN

25. Pietrocola et. al. (2014 Apr 25). Coffee induces autophagy in vivo. Retrieved from https://www.ncbi.nlm.nih.gov/pubmed/24769862

26. Hong-Feng et. al. (2014 November 13). Epigallocatechin-3-Gallate Attenuates Impairment of Learning and Memory in Chronic Unpredictable Mild Stress-Treated Rats by Restoring Hippocampal Autophagic Flux. Retrieved from https://www.ncbi.nlm.nih.gov/pmc/articles/PMC4231069/

27. Finn PF, Dice JF. (2005 May 9). Ketone bodies stimulate chaperone-mediated autophagy.. Retrieved from https://www.ncbi.nlm.nih.gov/pubmed/15883160

28. Thyagarajan et. al. (2010). Triterpenes from Ganoderma Lucidum induce autophagy in colon cancer through the inhibition of p38 mitogen-activated kinase (p38 MAPK). Retrieved from https://www.ncbi.nlm.nih.gov/pubmed/20574924

29. Hung et. al. (2009 October 28). 6-Shogaol, an active constituent of dietary ginger, induces autophagy by inhibiting the AKT/mTOR pathway in human non-small cell lung cancer A549 cells. Retrieved from https://www.ncbi.nlm.nih.gov/pubmed/19799425

30. Wang et. al. (2016 December 9). Curcumin protects neuronal cells against status-epilepticus-induced hippocampal damage through induction of autophagy and

inhibition of necroptosis. Retrieved from https://www.ncbi.nlm.nih.gov/pubmed/28177687

31. Li et. al. 2016 July 27. Galangin Induces Autophagy via Deacetylation of LC3 by SIRT1 in HepG2 Cells. Retrieved from https://www.ncbi.nlm.nih.gov/pubmed/27460655

32. Jo et. al. (2014 Jun 18). Sulforaphane induces autophagy through ERK activation in neuronal cells. Retrieved from https://www.ncbi.nlm.nih.gov/pubmed/24952354

33. Lee, Jeong, Park. (2014 October 10). Sulforaphane-induced autophagy flux prevents prion protein-mediated neurotoxicity through AMPK pathway. Retrieved from https://www.ncbi.nlm.nih.gov/pubmed/25130556

34. Author unkown. (2010 August 23). Eating berries may activate the brain's natural housekeeper for healthy aging. Retrieved from https://www.acs.org/content/acs/en/pressroom/newsreleases/2010/august/eating-berries-may-activate-the-brains-natural-housekeeper-for-healthy-aging.html

35. Jing-Lan et. al. (2018 January 9). Pterostilbene inhibits reactive oxygen species production and apoptosis in primary spinal cord neurons by activating autophagy via the mechanistic target of rapamycin signaling pathway. Retrieved from https://www.ncbi.nlm.nih.gov/pmc/articles/PMC5802216/

36. Shin et. al. 2013 June 10. The omega-3 polyunsaturated fatty acid DHA induces simultaneous apoptosis and autophagy via mitochondrial ROS-mediated Akt-mTOR

signaling in prostate cancer cells expressing mutant p53. Retrieved from https://www.ncbi.nlm.nih.gov/pubmed/23841076

37. Hanjani, Nazanin Asghari and Vafa, Mohammadreza. (2018 June 29). Protein Restriction, Epigenetic Diet, Intermittent Fasting as New Approaches for Preventing Age-associated Diseases. Retrieved from https://www.ncbi.nlm.nih.gov/pmc/articles/PMC6036773/

38. Bonfili et. al. (2017 May 25). Microbiota modulation counteracts Alzheimer's disease progression influencing neuronal proteolysis and gut hormones plasma levels. Retrieved from https://www.nature.com/articles/s41598-017-02587-2

39. Liu et. al. (2015 Jan 28). Long-term treatment with Ginkgo biloba extract EGb 761 improves symptoms and pathology in a transgenic mouse model of Alzheimer's disease. Retrieved from https://www.ncbi.nlm.nih.gov/pubmed/25637484

40. Yuying et. al. (2016 Oct. 28). Identification of natural products with neuronal and metabolic benefits through autophagy induction. Retrieved from https://www.ncbi.nlm.nih.gov/pmc/articles/PMC5240827/

41. Shaoping Wu, Ph.D. and Jun Sun, Ph.D. (2011 Apr. 11). Vitamin D, Vitamin D Receptor, and Macroautophagy in Inflammation and Infection. Retrieved from https://www.ncbi.nlm.nih.gov/pmc/articles/PMC3285235/

42. Høyer-Hansen, Nordbrandt, Jäättelä. (2010 May 19). Autophagy as a basis for the health-promoting effects of vitamin D. https://www.cell.com/trends/molecular-medicine/pdf/S1471-4914(10)00056-0.pdf?code=cell-site

43. Jin et. al. (2018 January). Carnitine induces autophagy and restores high-fat diet-induced mitochondrial dysfunction. Retrieved from https://www.metabolismjournal.com/article/S0026-0495(17)30249-4/pdf

44. Enomoto et. al. (2007 Dec.) Vitamin K2-induced cell growth inhibition via autophagy formation in cholangiocellular carcinoma cell lines. https://www.ncbi.nlm.nih.gov/pubmed/17982686

45. Armstrong et. al. (2015 June). Exploiting Cannabinoid-Induced Cytotoxic Autophagy to Drive Melanoma Cell Death. Retrieved from https://www.sciencedirect.com/science/article/pii/S0022202X15372870

46. Sarkar et. al. (2005 Sep. 26). Lithium induces autophagy by inhibiting inositol monophosphatase. Retrieved from https://www.ncbi.nlm.nih.gov/pubmed/16186256

47. Qichun et. al. (2016 Feb. 15). Pharmacologic preconditioning with berberine attenuating ischemia-induced apoptosis and promoting autophagy in neuron. Retrieved from https://www.ncbi.nlm.nih.gov/pmc/articles/PMC4846963/

48. McCarty, DiNicolantonio, O'Keefe. (2015 Aug. 10).Retrieved from https://www.ncbi.nlm.nih.gov/pubmed/26306884

49. Arabit et. al. (2018 June 10). Rhodiola rosea Improves Lifespan, Locomotion, and Neurodegeneration in a Drosophila melanogaster Model of Huntington's Disease. Retrieved from https://www.ncbi.nlm.nih.gov/pmc/articles/PMC6015705/

50. Jinghui et. al. (2018 May 1). Metabolomics study of the therapeutic mechanism of Schisandra chinensis lignans on aging rats induced by d-galactose. Retrieved from https://www.ncbi.nlm.nih.gov/pmc/articles/PMC5935080/

51. Guo et. al. (2018 March 21). Resveratrol protects early brain injury after subarachnoid hemorrhage by activating autophagy and inhibiting apoptosis mediated by the Akt/mTOR pathway. Retrieved from https://journals.lww.com/neuroreport/Fulltext/2018/03020/Resveratrol_protects_early_brain_injury_after.6.aspx

52. Sigrist et. al. (2013 Nov. 15). Spermidine-triggered autophagy ameliorates memory during aging. Retrieved from https://www.tandfonline.com/doi/pdf/10.4161/auto.26918

53. Sara Lindberg. (2018 Aug. 23). Autophagy: What You Need to Know. Retrieved from https://www.healthline.com/health/autophagy#diet

54. Fung, Jason. (2016 Oct. 5). How to renew your body: Fasting and autophagy. Retrieved from

https://www.dietdoctor.com/renew-body-fasting-autophagy

55. Zauner et. al. (2000 June). Resting energy expenditure in short-term starvation is increased as a result of an increase in serum norepinephrine. Retrieved from https://www.ncbi.nlm.nih.gov/pubmed/10837292

56. van Praag, Fleshner, Schwartz, and Mattson. (2014 Nov. 12). Exercise, Energy Intake, Glucose Homeostasis, and the Brain. Retrieved from https://www.jneurosci.org/content/34/46/15139

57. Lee, Seroogy, Mattson. (2002 Jan. 21). Dietary restriction enhances neurotrophin expression and neurogenesis in the hippocampus of adult mice. Retrieved from https://onlinelibrary.wiley.com/doi/full/10.1046/j.0022-3042.2001.00747.x

58. Anton et. al. (2017 Oct. 31). Flipping the Metabolic Switch: Understanding and Applying Health Benefits of Fasting. Retrieved from https://www.ncbi.nlm.nih.gov/pmc/articles/PMC5783752/

59. Alirezaei et. al. (2010 Aug. 16). Short-term fasting induces profound neuronal autophagy. Retrieved from https://www.tandfonline.com/doi/abs/10.4161/auto.6.6.12376

60. Hartman et. al. (1992 April 1). Augmented growth hormone (GH) secretory burst frequency and amplitude mediate enhanced GH secretion during a two-day fast in

normal men. Retrieved from https://academic.oup.com/jcem/article-abstract/74/4/757/3004645?redirectedFrom=fulltext

61. Navpreet Amole, Suraj Unniappan. (2009 March). Fasting induces preproghrelin mRNA expression in the brain and gut of zebrafish, Danio rerio. Retrieved from https://www.sciencedirect.com/science/article/pii/S0016648008004000

62. S. Klein, Y. Sakurai, J. A. Romijn, and R. M. Carroll. (1993 Nov. 1). Progressive alterations in lipid and glucose metabolism during short-term fasting in young adult men. Retrieved from https://www.physiology.org/doi/abs/10.1152/ajpendo.1993.265.5.E801

63. Cheng et. al. (2014 June). Prolonged fasting reduces IGF-1/PKA to promote hematopoietic-stem-cell-based regeneration and reverse immunosuppression. Retrieved from https://www.ncbi.nlm.nih.gov/pubmed/24905167

64. Mattson et. al. (Intermittent metabolic switching, neuroplasticity and brain health. Retrieved from https://www.ncbi.nlm.nih.gov/pmc/articles/PMC5913738/

65. Ayano et. al. (2016 Jan. 6). Mammalian autophagy is essential for hepatic and renal ketogenesis during starvation. Retrieved from https://www.nature.com/articles/srep18944

66. McCarty, DiNicolantonio, O'Keefe. (2015 Aug. 10). Ketosis may promote brain macroautophagy by activating

Sirt1 and hypoxia-inducible factor-1. Retrieved from https://www.ncbi.nlm.nih.gov/pubmed/26306884

67. Patrick F. Finn and J. Fred Dice. (2005 May 9). Ketone Bodies Stimulate Chaperone-mediated Autophagy. Retrieved from http://www.jbc.org/content/280/27/25864.full

68. Campos et. al. (2018 Aug. 7). Exercise prevents impaired autophagy and proteostasis in a model of neurogenic myopathy. Retrieved from https://www.nature.com/articles/s41598-018-30365-1

69. Campos et. al. (2017 Aug. 3). Exercise reestablishes autophagic flux and mitochondrial quality control in heart failure. Retrieved from https://www.ncbi.nlm.nih.gov/pubmed/28598232

70. André Julião. (2018 Sep. 26). Physical exercise improves the elimination of toxic proteins from muscles. Retrieved from http://agencia.fapesp.br/physical-exercise-improves-the-elimination-of-toxic-proteins-from-muscles/28788/

71. Sagrillo-Fagundes, Bienvenue-Pariseault, Vaillancourt. (2019 January 10). Melatonin: The smart molecule that differentially modulates autophagy in tumor and normal placental cells. Retrieved from https://journals.plos.org/plosone/article?id=10.1371/journal.pone.0202458

72. Van Cauter E, Plat L. (1996 May). Physiology of growth hormone secretion during sleep. Retrieved from https://www.ncbi.nlm.nih.gov/pubmed/8627466

73. Kenneth Maiese. (2017 Sep. 16). Moving to the Rhythm with Clock (Circadian) Genes, Autophagy, mTOR, and SIRT1 in Degenerative Disease and Cancer. Retrieved from https://www.ncbi.nlm.nih.gov/pmc/articles/PMC5600856/

74. Ma D, Panda S, Lin JD. (2011 Sep. 6). Temporal orchestration of circadian autophagy rhythm by C/EBPβ. Retrieved from https://www.ncbi.nlm.nih.gov/pubmed/21897364

75. Valter D. Longo and Satchidananda Panda. (2016 June 14). Fasting, circadian rhythms, and time restricted feeding in healthy lifespan. Retrieved from https://www.ncbi.nlm.nih.gov/pmc/articles/PMC5388543/

76. Shubhroz Gill and Satchidananda Panda. (2015 Sep. 24). A smartphone app reveals erratic diurnal eating patterns in humans that can be modulated for health benefits. Retrieved from https://www.ncbi.nlm.nih.gov/pmc/articles/PMC4635036/

77. Antoni, Johnston, Collins, and Robertson. (2014 March 26). The Effects of Intermittent Energy Restriction on Indices of Cardiometabolic Health. Retrieved from https://ibimapublishing.com/articles/ENDO/2014/459119/

78. Hutchison et. al. (2019 April 19). Time-Restricted Feeding Improves Glucose Tolerance in Men at Risk for Type 2 Diabetes: A Randomized Crossover Trial. Retrieved from https://onlinelibrary.wiley.com/doi/abs/10.1002/oby.22449

79. Cauter, Polonsky, Scheen. (1997 Oct. 1). Roles of Circadian Rhythmicity and Sleep in Human Glucose Regulation. Retrieved from https://academic.oup.com/edrv/article/18/5/716/2530790

80. Mulder, Nagorny, Lyssenko, Groop. (2009 Jul.). Melatonin receptors in pancreatic islets: good morning to a novel type 2 diabetes gene. Retrieved from https://www.ncbi.nlm.nih.gov/pubmed/19377888

81. Penke et. al. (2018 Jan 22). Heat Shock Proteins and Autophagy Pathways in Neuroprotection: From Molecular Bases to Pharmacological Interventions. Retrieved from https://www.ncbi.nlm.nih.gov/pmc/articles/PMC5796267/

82. The JAMA Network Journals. (2015, February 23). Sauna use associated with reduced risk of cardiac, all-cause mortality. ScienceDaily. Retrieved September 25, 2019 from www.sciencedaily.com/releases/2015/02/150223122602.htm

83. Laukkanen et. al. (2017 March). Sauna bathing is inversely associated with dementia and Alzheimer's disease in middle-aged Finnish men. Retrieved from https://academic.oup.com/ageing/article/46/2/245/2654230

84. M.GabriellaSantoro. (1999 June). Heat shock factors and the control of the stress response. Retrieved from https://www.sciencedirect.com/science/article/abs/pii/S0006295299002993?via%3Dihub

85. Yang, Xing, Zhou, Chen. (2010 Mar 30). Mitochondrial autophagy protects against heat shock-induced apoptosis through reducing cytosolic cytochrome c release and downstream caspase-3 activation. Retrieved from https://www.ncbi.nlm.nih.gov/pubmed/20361931

86. Ho et. al. (1988 April). Fasting enhances growth hormone secretion and amplifies the complex rhythms of growth hormone secretion in man. Retrieved from https://www.ncbi.nlm.nih.gov/pmc/articles/PMC329619/

87. Ting-Ting et. al. (2017 March). Stress injuries and autophagy in mouse hippocampus after chronic cold exposure. Retrieved from https://www.ncbi.nlm.nih.gov/pmc/articles/PMC5399722/

88. Lage, Surowiak, Holm. (2008 November). YB-1 as a potential target in cancer therapy. Retrieved from https://www.ncbi.nlm.nih.gov/pubmed/18773210

89. Siems, van Kuijk, Maass, Brenke. (1994 March). Uric acid and glutathione levels during short-term whole body cold exposure. Retrieved from https://www.ncbi.nlm.nih.gov/pubmed/8063192

90. Lichtenbelt et. al. (2009 April 9). Cold-Activated Brown Adipose Tissue in Healthy Men. Retrieved from https://www.nejm.org/doi/full/10.1056/nejmoa0808718

91. Imbeault, Dépault, Haman. (2009 April). Cold exposure increases adiponectin levels in men. Retrieved from https://www.ncbi.nlm.nih.gov/pubmed/19303978

92. Hirvonen et. al. (2006 May). Effectiveness of different cryotherapies on pain and disease activity in active rheumatoid arthritis. A randomised single blinded controlled trial. Retrieved from https://www.ncbi.nlm.nih.gov/pubmed/16870097

93. Nivon et. al. (2009 Aug 20). Autophagy activation by NFkappaB is essential for cell survival after heat shock. Retrieved from https://www.ncbi.nlm.nih.gov/pubmed/19502777/

94. Tanida, Minematsu-Ikeguchi, Ueno, Kominami. (2005 July 31). Lysosomal turnover, but not a cellular level, of endogenous LC3 is a marker for autophagy. Retrieved from https://www.ncbi.nlm.nih.gov/pubmed/16874052/

www.ingramcontent.com/pod-product-compliance
Lightning Source LLC
Chambersburg PA
CBHW052057110526
44591CB00013B/2249